GOD AND MONEY

HOW WE DISCOVERED
TRUE RICHES
AT HARVARD BUSINESS SCHOOL

JOHN CORTINES

GREGORY BAUMER

R✺SE
PUBLISHING
Carson, California

God and Money:
How We Discovered True Riches
at Harvard Business School
© 2016 John Cortines and Gregory Baumer
Rose Publishing, Inc.
17909 Adria Maru Lane
Carson, California 90746 U.S.A.
Email: info@rose-publishing.com
www.rose-publishing.com

Unless otherwise noted, Scripture quotations are from The Holy Bible, English Standard Version® (ESV®), copyright © 2001 by Crossway, a publishing ministry of Good News Publishers. Used by permission. All rights reserved.

Scripture quotations marked (NIV) are taken from the Holy Bible, New International Version®, NIV®. Copyright © 1973, 1978, 1984, 2011 by Biblica, Inc.™ Used by permission of Zondervan. All rights reserved worldwide. www.zondervan.com The "NIV" and "New International Version" are trademarks registered in the United States Patent and Trademark Office by Biblica, Inc.™

Rose Publishing is in no way liable for any context, change of content, or activity for the websites listed. Inclusion of a work does not necessarily mean endorsement of all its contents or of other works by the same author(s).

Cover design by Kent Jensen. Book design by Sergio Urquiza.

Hardcover ISBN: 9781628624076, Paperback ISBN: 9781628624731

Library of Congress Cataloging-in-Publication Data

Names: Baumer, Gregory, author.
Title: God and money : how we discovered true riches at Harvard Business
    School / Gregory Baumer and John Cortines.
Description: Carson : Rose Publishing, Inc., 2016.
Identifiers: LCCN 2015046944 (print) | LCCN 2015048579 (ebook) | ISBN
    9781628624076 | ISBN 9781628624083 ()
Subjects: LCSH: Christian giving. | Generosity–Religious
    aspects–Christianity. | Wealth–Religious aspects–Christianity. |
    Money–Religious aspects–Christianity.
Classification: LCC BV772 .B34 2016 (print) | LCC BV772 (ebook) | DDC
    241/.68–dc23
LC record available at http://lccn.loc.gov/2015046944

Printed in the United States of America
030816RRD

To our wives, who supported us through the book-writing process with boundless patience and grace. Alison and Megan, this book wouldn't exist without you.

Every idea in this book bears your fingerprints, thanks to your willingness to travel on this journey with us. We each look forward to lives spent serving Christ with you at our sides.

Contents

FOREWORD

I first met John Cortines and Greg Baumer in a phone appointment. They contacted me to ask my advice on some ideas surrounding their proposed book, which has now become a reality.

I later had the privilege of meeting them at a Generous Giving "Celebration of Generosity" Conference. Then I heard them speak . . . and absolutely loved what they had to say.

I consider it a privilege to encourage young men who are passionate for Christ and His Word. When Greg and John told me they'd been touched by my books *Money, Possessions, and Eternity* and *The Treasure Principle*, I was humbled and grateful. But what makes me really excited about their book is their desire to influence a younger generation concerning generous giving, challenging their peers to look beyond our unparalleled standard of living to a calling higher than ourselves.

Like many people, I find there are far more demands on my time than I can accommodate. But because of my passion for the message of stewarding God's money, when they asked me to write the foreword to this book, I couldn't pass up the opportunity. I do this gladly, smiling at God's gracious work in raising up strategic generous givers in every generation.

Many of us have drawn attention to the fact that it's older generations who give away larger portions of their income to God's work. The younger generation, even those who give more of their time, often give less of their money. I pray God will use Greg and John to inspire their millennial generation to take seriously the path of generosity. With the transference of wealth from one generation to the next, and the rising up of young entrepreneurs and enthusiastic Christ-centered servants, God is creating a fresh company of people to unleash an outpouring of generosity. I pray—and fully expect—that God will use *God and Money* as part of this.

John and Greg realize what everyone should know—that middle-class Americans are among the richest people in world history.

It's time for Christ-followers to understand that God has bigger purposes than increasing our standard of living—He wants us to increase our standard of giving.

I long, as do these two young men, to help people understand that glorifying God in how we use our money isn't just a duty, it's a delight! There's simply no greater joy than giving. All people seek happiness because that's how our happy God created us. But that happiness can only be found in God's blueprint for living. In the only statement of Jesus in the book of Acts that's not in the Gospels, we learn that our Lord said, "It is more blessed [*makarios*, happy-making] to give than to receive" (Acts 20:35). There it is. Give, and God will bring you an addictive happiness that will prompt you to go on giving. Give more and more not only so that you'll help others and please God, but so that you'll be happier than you ever imagined you could be! This isn't prosperity theology—it's pure Jesus-honoring delight!

John and Greg propose principles for Christ-centered generosity, while documenting that this generosity promotes physical and emotional well-being. Drawing on their surveys and interviews of wealthy Christians, they present some surprising examples of open-handedness that honors our Savior and King.

The authors are on a mission to influence modern Christians in generous giving. *God and Money* can contribute greatly to this worthy end.

Those who are convinced by God's Word and the work of the Holy Spirit to put Christian generosity not at the fringes, but at the center of their financial plans, will welcome this book. Those unsure of God's desires and callings to them will benefit greatly from it, providing they open their hearts to whatever God has for them as they read. (If you refuse to open your heart to God, this book isn't for you; but start it anyway and see what God does to your heart!)

I commend John and Greg for their eternal perspective, and their passion for helping us open our eyes to what really matters, and will matter forever. *God and Money* is a refreshing book, all the more because of the genuine and heartfelt commitment of its authors. But what I love most is that its focus is on the big picture—not treasures on earth, that will turn to dust, but treasures in Heaven, that will last forever. May we live here and now so as to make a difference then and there!

Randy Alcorn
June, 2015

PREFACE

"To give largely and liberally, not grudging at all,
requires a new heart."

—R. M. McCheyne, 19th-century Scottish pastor

God loves us. He wants the best for us. And He knows that we thrive when we give ourselves away. Thus, He calls us to be givers—not tithers, not donors, but radical, all-in givers.

We did not always understand this, and in some ways we're still learning it, and relearning it over and over. But this book is about our ongoing journey from mindsets of *Spending* (Greg) and *Saving* (John) to the mindset of *Servant*. We have learned so much along this journey, but most significantly, we no longer ask "How much should we give?" Rather, our question has now become, "How much do we need to keep?"

On our journey, we've found that there is power in specifics. So you'll see that we give specific numbers when we refer to our own spending, and to net worth or "finish lines" (more about this in Part II). We do so in the hope that these specifics will be illuminating. It's certainly not meant to be prescriptive. We do think, however, that each person should prayerfully consider becoming *self-prescriptive*—establishing financial rules of life and finish lines that they live out in community, with accountability. There is freedom in such boundaries.

At the start of our time at Harvard Business School, we each had plans to buy multi-million dollar houses, accumulate fortunes for ourselves, and yes, perhaps give to our churches and some charities along the way. John's online banking password was "Retire_at_40"! Now, however, we've pledged to give away all of our financial earnings beyond certain thresholds we have prayerfully established. We believe this is a healthy response to what the Bible has to say about wealth, and we give all of the credit and praise to God for taking us on this journey. It has been a hard one, but one in which His faithfulness, sovereignty, and boundless love have been made crystal clear in our lives. We now have some insulation from all the stress and anxiety (and sin) that money often causes. Our lives have been enriched in every way by embracing a new way of thinking about wealth—a way that first and foremost seeks to bring glory to God through our finances. We're thankful to know Him. We're thankful for newfound joy and peace that has become tangible in our daily lives!

Our theological backgrounds, if you care to know, are fairly conservatively evangelical. In writing this book our goal has been to stay close to Scripture, and we attempt to reference relevant verses when possible. However, we also have backgrounds in finance (Greg) and engineering (John), and strive to bring empirical rigor and modern financial analysis into the mix as well. The result, we hope, is something that honors the best in the culture around us, engages with sociology and philosophy, adheres to the Scriptures, and finally brings a deep challenge to the heart of every Christian.

We believe that this book is a small part of a large movement. In fact, through our research we've become convinced that our generation stands poised to witness a groundswell of generosity unlike anything the world has ever seen. We pray that it will happen!

To illuminate this growing trend and bring the principles we'll explore to life, we will dive deep into the stories of five families in the chapters ahead. They will appear throughout the book, putting a human face on the concepts we'll explore together. Because they revealed sensitive personal information we have changed their names and cities, but all other details, such as their jobs and actual dollar amounts appearing in the stories, remain unaltered. We hope your journey through this book will be uplifting and challenging, freeing and convicting. It has been all of these things for us.

John Cortines and Gregory Baumer
Boston, MA
April, 2015

ACKNOWLEDGEMENTS

This book did not come to exist in a vacuum. Countless leaders have come before, placing trail markers that we have followed on our journey. Without them we would have certainly gotten lost in the woods! We want to take a moment to say thank you to several key individuals, knowing that many more will remain unmentioned.

To Harvey Cox, for bold leadership and scholarship for Christ, and for teaching well into his eighties so that we could benefit from his keen insights at Harvard Divinity School in the Fall of 2014.

To our case studies, who remain anonymous, for living lives of radical generosity and being willing to share openly with us about very personal matters.

To 200-plus business leaders who answered our survey on Wealth and Giving, providing a rich data set to explore and investigate at the genesis of this project.

To Todd Harper, Matt Mancinelli, John Esler, and Mark MacDonald, who we met in the upper room of the Red House restaurant in Cambridge, Massachusetts on a snowy day that impacted our lives forever.

To Derek van Bever, our advisor at Harvard Business School, for challenging us to take our book to the next level.

To our Board of Directors for Life—Walker and Ida Brumskine, Matt and Paige Deimund, Dylan and Tas Emmett, Paul and Emmalee Kalmbach, Andrew and Christy Mawdsley—thank you for becoming a living definition of true Christian fellowship in our lives.

To those who spoke great wisdom and blessed us on our journey: Randy Alcorn, Tony Cimmarrusti, Julie Wilson, Pat Combes, Al Mueller, Tim Sullivan, Grace Nicollete, Troy Austin, Will Messenger, Pastor David Self, Tyler Self, David Wills, Rob West, Jeff Barneson, Catherine Muthey, Pastor David Swaim, Scott Rice,

Graham and April Smith, and Ron Blue.

To the countless authors and scholars, from John Chrysostom 1,600 years ago, to Christian Smith at Notre Dame today, who have woven a consistent narrative of Christian thinking, warning against the dangers of self-centeredness and calling us toward the abundant life of generosity. Your books helped change our lives.

To the dozens of selfless individuals who ran and participated in study groups for our prereleased book in 2015. Your insightful feedback helped make the book you hold in your hands exponentially better! Thank you for digging in with us and wrestling with the content of this manuscript.

To our literary partners, Amanda Bray and Dan Balow. You each helped us go from clueless beginners to something that might pass for authors, and we're forever indebted for this.

To our theological auditor, Professor Rob Plummer at Southern Baptist Theological Seminary. Your keen eye ensured that we stayed faithful to an evangelical reading of the Bible, and we're ever so grateful.

We are grateful to you all for your generosity toward us.

INTRODUCTION

"How we relate to money is a central issue of discipleship. I think this is a topic that is really under-focused on in the church. Greed and stewardship seem to be glossed over, as 'too personal' to touch from the pulpit. I think it should be a much more focal part of the church's message."

"Giving generously is one of the most profound and impactful spiritual practices I have encountered."

"Awesome topic, even completing this survey compels me to pray about this more."

"I have realized there isn't lot of good guidance available on this topic."

All of these quotes are responses to a survey on Christian wealth and giving. We conducted the survey in the fall of 2014 as part of a class at Harvard Divinity School called "God and Money." These statements demonstrate that God's people are hungry for more discussion on the topic of generosity. We have been fortunate to speak with and learn from many incredibly generous Christians in the course of researching this book. We have synthesized our findings into a framework for generosity that we plan to use in our own lives, and our hope is that it might prove uplifting and freeing for others as well. Our ultimate aim is to provide an actionable approach to making real decisions around wealth and giving, with God's teaching on the subject as its firm foundation. Much has been written about the right principles and attitudes we should apply to giving. However, for whatever reason, many Christians do not actually apply these principles in their lives.

Our hope is to apply those often neglected principles to create a very practical, pragmatic framework for making the real-life decisions that most Western Christians will have to make. We believe that thinking about these issues early on, rather than after wealth has already been obtained, makes the decision to live according to godly principles that much easier. Indeed, as one survey respondent put it, "early decisions on money, charity, and possessions establish a personal values trajectory, and become hard to revise." Most

Christians agree we should be grateful to God for the material blessings He has given us, and most of us agree we should be generous with our material wealth to help others. That is uncontroversial. Where it gets difficult is actually applying those concepts to real-world decisions. For example, how should a 21st-century Christian think about buying a house? How "nice" of a house can a Christian buy without crossing the principles of gratitude and generosity to which he knows he should adhere?

Decisions like this are difficult to make because they involve so many factors—faith, to be sure, but also the desire to provide for one's family, to ensure safety for one's children, etc. This book is intended to help answer questions such as these. It is intended to evaluate the more granular wealth-and-giving issues of Christian life. By the way, in this book we use the terms "money," "wealth," and "possessions" interchangeably. As you will read, we believe that all of our material provision should be used to honor God, not just our "excess." So when we use any of these terms, we are referring comprehensively to all material and financial assets God has provided in our lives.

We also want to clearly state that financial giving is just one component of the Body of Christ's work. Each member of the Church is called to serve. Those who have earthly riches have no special standing or cause for pride. Some can give money, some can give hard work, and some can give leadership direction, but we are all equal brothers and sisters in the Lord, humbly bringing whatever we have to offer to the Body of Christ for His glory. We have often heard it said in churches that discussing actual dollar figures is not helpful, because it is the heart that matters rather than the number of zeros on a check. While this is mostly true, it often forces Christians to make financial decisions of great importance without outside counsel, and can even lead to the temptation to embrace the theory of "giving as we feel led" but then never quite feeling the urge! We acknowledge the primacy of the heart, but want to also state clearly: Actions matter, and amounts matter! Let's begin an honest dialogue to discover the heart of Christ where our financial rubber meets the road.

PART I: FOUNDATIONS

CHAPTER ONE

Wealth and Giving in the Bible

*"You shall remember the L*ord* your God, for it is he who gives you the power to get wealth."*
—Deuteronomy 8:18[1]

In my first year at Harvard Business School, I (Greg) read the entire Bible front to back. Although I grew up in the church, this was my first time reading every word of Scripture in order. Reading the whole Bible as a single unit allowed me to better appreciate the overall flow of God's story: God creates man, who rebels against Him. God relentlessly pursues His people, only to be betrayed over and over again. In His faithfulness, God sends His son Jesus Christ to bear the colossal consequences of our sin. In the resurrection of Jesus, God demonstrates His victory over sin, offering us the opportunity to enter into pure relationship with Him. Now free of our sin, we identify our ultimate purpose: "to glorify God, and to enjoy Him forever."[2] Reading the entire

---

1 Bible passages throughout this book are quoted from the English Standard Version, unless otherwise noted.

2 From the Westminster Shorter Catechism. http://www.westminsterconfession.org/confessional-standards/the-westminster-shorter-catechism.php. Accessed 3/4/15.

Bible made clear to me that God's story is one of faithfulness, salvation, and grace.

I noticed a few other common threads in the Bible's narrative during this experience as well. For one thing, the Bible says *a lot* about money. The Bible includes approximately 500 verses on both prayer and faith, but more than 2,000 verses on money![3] Indeed, money is the subject of roughly 40 percent of Jesus' parables. I thought God must consider the topic to be quite important to devote so much space to the subject. So when John and I began exploring the topic of wealth and generosity in more depth, I wondered, "What does the Bible *really* say about money?" Is there a way to identify Scripture's overall lessons on the subject? I started digging into those 2,000 verses and was amazed to find that God does indeed teach a consistent set of lessons about wealth and giving, from Genesis to Revelation.

For a Closer Look . . .

In 1973, businessman Howard Dayton categorized all 2,350 verses on money into a single, topical index. As he told us, "That study radically and permanently changed me from worshiping money to serving Christ." Having served as the leader of both Crown Financial and Compass Ministries, Howard has helped reach over 50 million people with biblical truth about money. To view the index yourself, see "Compass: 2,350 Verses on Money" at GodandMoney.net/resources.

In this chapter we explore several of the most critical passages regarding wealth and money in Scripture. We devote our first chapter to understanding God's teaching on this subject because we believe the Bible should be a primary resource for gaining

---

3   Laurie, Greg; "Money & Motives." http://www.oneplace.com/ministries/a-new-beginning/read/articles/money-and-motives-9220.html. Accessed 11/18/14.

an appropriate understanding of any subject, including money and wealth. By attempting to place our whole book on the firm foundation of God's Word, we hope to build a perspective that honors God's truth above all else.

Two qualifiers before we begin. First, neither of us are trained biblical scholars. We do not attempt to present any new interpretations of Scripture in this book. Rather, our goal is to summarize the Bible's key lessons on money, wealth, and generosity as commonly understood and interpreted by the Church today. To help us accomplish this goal, we partnered with Dr. Robert Plummer, Chairman of the New Testament Department and Professor of New Testament Interpretation at Southern Baptist Theological Seminary in Louisville, Kentucky. Dr. Plummer graciously reviewed our discussion of God's Word throughout chapters one and two to ensure we analyzed and interpreted each passage as faithfully as possible. We are very grateful for his support.

Second, this chapter covers only a small fraction of the Bible's teaching on wealth and giving. We have selected a sample of passages from each section of Scripture that we believe exemplify the Bible's overall lessons on wealth and giving. See the adjacent box for a comprehensive topical index of biblical money verses.

OK, let's dive in!

WEALTH AND GIVING IN THE OLD TESTAMENT

> *"If you pour yourself out for the hungry and satisfy the desire of the afflicted, then shall your light rise in the darkness and your gloom be as the noonday."*
> —Isaiah 58:10

14

THE PATRIARCHS

We began our research by exploring wealth and giving in the Old Testament prior to the institution of the Mosaic Law, specifically studying the stories of Cain and Abel, Abraham, and Jacob. The question at stake in these passages is to what extent money was a factor in the patriarchs' relationship with God prior to the institution of specific commands regarding wealth and giving in the Mosaic Law. What lessons about wealth and giving can we learn from the fathers of our faith, who looked forward to and longed for the eventual fulfillment of God's promises we now know as New Covenant believers?[4]

Cain and Abel (Genesis 4:3-7): Both Cain and Abel present offerings to the Lord. The Lord "had regard" for Abel and his offering, but "for Cain and his offering [the Lord] had no regard." Hebrews 11:4 explains that "By faith Abel offered to God a more acceptable sacrifice than Cain." Cain and Abel appear to be giving voluntarily, and their gifts were judged based on faith, not on quantity.[5] Faith is a response to God's gracious self-revelation, and we don't know exactly how Abel's offering was a more acceptable response to what God had revealed. It is often suggested that Abel's offering of a blood sacrifice was superior to the agricultural products offered by Cain. Regardless of the specific details (now a matter of conjecture), Cain's bitter resentment at God's rebuke reveal the true state of his heart toward God.

Abraham (Genesis 14:18-24): Abraham has just defeated Chedorlaomer, who had previously attacked and robbed Abraham's kinsman, Lot. Upon his return to Salem (i.e., Jerusalem), Abraham gives 10 percent of the spoils to Melchizedek, Priest of the God

---

4 Hebrews 11:13; Romans 4:1-3

5 Croteau, David A., *You Mean I Don't Have to Tithe?* (McMaster Theological Studies), 87.

Most High.[6] This gift also appears to be voluntary, as opposed to an act of obedience to a specific command. Abraham confirms this conclusion when he states that he had previously vowed not to keep any spoils from the battle; indeed, Abraham proceeds to give away the remaining 90 percent of the treasure to his compatriots shortly thereafter. Moreover, Abraham appears to view the spoils as belonging to God, not himself. Here we see the first instance of recognition that all the resources God blesses us with truly belong to Him!

Jacob (Genesis 28:13-22): God promises to remain by Jacob's side, as well as to provide Jacob with land and a great number of descendants who will bless the earth. Jacob responds conditionally: *if* God does these things, *then* Yahweh will be his God and he will give God one tenth of his possessions. Jacob shows he is actually quite fearful and insecure in God's promises. (Many stories in Scripture remind us how gracious God is to redeem and use weak, faltering, and frequently mistaken saints—people like us!) Jacob proceeds to spend 20 years with his uncle Laban before returning to the land God had promised, and the biblical text does not mention Jacob offering any gifts to God during that intervening period.[7] Jacob apparently exhibits a tit-for-tat attitude toward God that is all too common in the human heart.

The Mosaic Law

The prior section illustrates that wealth and money were highly relevant to the Patriarchs' relationship with God, even if God had not yet issued specific commands related to wealth.[8] It is

---

6 That Abraham's gift to Melchizedek was merely a portion of the spoils, and not a "tithe" on Abraham's entire wealth, is confirmed in Hebrews 7:4.

7 Croteau, *You Mean I Don't Have to Tithe?*, 93.

8 Here is an interesting pre-Mosaic-Law anecdote for readers in the private equity or hedge fund industries. Some say the genesis of 20 percent as the conventional amount of carried interest earned by general partners is Joseph's solution to the famine in Genesis 47. Pharaoh would provide seed to the starving Egyptians, who would then grow crops. Eighty percent of the crops would belong to the Egyptians, while 20 percent would be paid to Pharaoh.

within the context of the Mosaic Law that God first delivers explicit commandments regarding wealth and giving, most famously through the institution of the tithe. The average Israelite in the Old Testament was actually commanded to give three distinct tithes:[9]

Levitical Tithe (Numbers 18:20-24): The Levitical Tithe was a 10-percent annual donation used to support the Levites. Unlike the other Israelite tribes, the Levites could not own land, and therefore received no inheritance. Thus, the Levitical Tithe was intended to serve as the Levites' inheritance, and was used to support their livelihood as temple servants, musicians, etc.[10]

Festival Tithe (Deuteronomy 12:17-19; 14:22-27; 26:10-16): The Festival Tithe was a 10-percent tithe used to host the Feast of Tabernacles, an annual festival honoring God's work in bringing the Israelites out of slavery in Egypt (Leviticus 23:42-43). Each individual Israelite actually maintained ownership of this tithe— they were commanded to "eat" the tithe themselves if the tithe was presented as animals or grain, or to use a monetary tithe to buy food for consumption during the festival.

Charity Tithe (Deuteronomy 14:28-29): The Charity Tithe was a 10-percent tithe offered in the third and sixth year of the Israelites' seven-year societal life cycle that was used to support foreigners, orphans, and widows, as well as to provide additional resources to the Levites.

As biblical scholar Craig Blomberg points out in *Neither Poverty nor Riches*, adding these three tithes together reveals that most Israelites donated approximately 23 percent of their income every year, not 10 percent, as is commonly taught in churches today

---

9 In addition to the three tithes paid by every Israelite, Levites paid a separate, fourth tithe to the priests.

10 Croteau, *You Mean I Don't Have to Tithe?*, 103.

(10-percent Levitical Tithe plus 10-percent Festival Tithe plus 10-percent Charity Tithe given two-out-of-seven years equals approximately 22.9 percent).[11] It is also worth highlighting that God intended one of these three tithes to be used to throw a giant festival! God desires that we use His gifts of provision for our own enjoyment, in addition to serving others.

Other Mosaic Law: The Mosaic Law contains several other commands regarding wealth and money beyond those specific to tithing, most of which relate to supporting the poor.

- Exodus 22 and 23 instruct the Israelites to ensure not just provision, but justice and opportunity for the poor: "Do not take advantage of an orphan or widow . . . Do not deny justice to your poor in their lawsuits . . ."

- Leviticus 25 contains a host of directives intended to protect and support the poor, including the Year of Jubilee and mechanisms for redeeming families who have lost their property. The Year of Jubilee was essentially an economic "reset button" pressed by Israelite society every 50 years. All land leases would end, with every family returning to the land of its inheritance, and all indentured servants would be freed from their masters.[12]

- Deuteronomy 15 articulates a series of commands related to caring for the poor, including direct commands to care for the poor in one's community. Many other passages in the Pentateuch present similar ideas. The theme is clear: wealth

---

11 Blomberg, *Neither Poverty nor Riches*, 89.

12 According to Professor Cox at Harvard Divinity School, some scholars doubt the Israelites actually obeyed the commands related to the Year of Jubilee. However, some evidence exists that the Israelites engaged in various forms of casuistry to avoid these commands. This continues today: in the 7th year, when the land is supposed to lie fallow, many grow food with hydroponics. Others technically "sell" their land to a Gentile for a year. See "In Israel, growing crops under biblical land laws" by Michele Chabin in USA Today at http://www.usatoday.com/story/news/world/2014/10/02/yom-kippur-israel-agriculture-fallow/16599363/.

is a gift from God, and one of the functions of wealth is to provide for one's community, especially the poor.

THE "CASE STUDIES"

These lessons related to wealth and money are represented by the lives of various biblical characters. The lives of biblical characters are most often studied from a broad perspective, with money being only tangential. When focusing directly on the monetary aspects of each story, however, new insights begin to emerge.

Boaz (Book of Ruth): Boaz, a wealthy landowner in Bethlehem, marries Ruth, a widow whose deceased husband was Boaz's relative.[13] Boaz treats Ruth, a foreigner and a widow, with incredible kindness, even before he knows he and Ruth are related. Their lives first intersect when Boaz allows poor immigrants to "glean" his land during the harvest. (In Leviticus 19:9-10 God commands the Israelites to leave the margins of their fields unharvested, thus providing a source of provision for the poor.) While one could construe Boaz's continued generosity toward Ruth as being driven by his growing personal interest in her, we can still learn much from Boaz's treatment of the poor in his community. Interestingly, the gleaning command in Leviticus 19 is placed within a sub-section of Scripture focusing on love of neighbor and is surrounded by other commands regarding stealing, oppression, and injustice. From Boaz's example we learn that one of the essential functions of wealth is to support "the least of these," and that maximizing one's own assets at the expense of those in need is an ungodly practice—on par with stealing, oppression, and injustice. God

---

13 The practice of marrying a deceased relative's widow is called Levirate Marriage and is mandated in Deuteronomy 25:5-6. The practice was intended to protect the widow and her children in a society where women lacked the ability to generate income on their own after the death of the husband. The Levirate Marriage could actually be avoided by performing a ritual called "halizah" described in Deuteronomy 25:9-10. According to the early church father Julius Africanus, the differences in Jesus' genealogies in Luke and Matthew are best explained by Levirate marriage. Where they diverge, one genealogy follow the legal line and one follows the biological line.

expects those of us blessed with plenty to actively serve the needs of the poor in our communities.[14]

David (1 & 2 Samuel; 1 Chronicles) and Solomon (2 Chronicles; 1 Kings): The record of King David's and King Solomon's use of wealth is quite mixed. On the one hand, both David and Solomon gained much of their wealth by exacting harsh tribute from nations David had defeated in battle. Indeed, David's bloody history at war was the reason God prohibited him from building God's temple in Jerusalem. On the other hand, both David and Solomon utilized their wealth to drive significant economic growth in Israel through capital investment and international trade. Moreover, David deeply desired to use his wealth in service of the Lord. His decision to donate significant personal wealth to the temple-building project, even after God barred him from building the temple himself, motivated a nationwide fundraiser that enabled Solomon to construct the temple. As Old Testament scholar Christopher Wright puts it, David "acknowledges the true source of all wealth (God Himself) and the comparative unworthiness of all human giving, which is merely giving back to God what already belongs to Him" (1 Chronicles 29:14).[15]

We can take much away from David and Solomon on the topic of wealth and money—both good and bad. We see that wealth can be obtained from unjust means; that wealth can drive economic activity and provide means of support for others in our communities; that wealth can enable much good but can also corrupt the heart; and that giving should by marked by "willingness, wholeheartedness, and joy, along with God-honoring worship, integrity, and honest intent."[16]

---

14   Wright, Christopher. "The Righteous Rich in the Old Testament." http://theotherjournal. com/2010/08/05/the-%E2%80%9Crighteous-rich%E2%80%9D-in-the-old-testament/. Accessed 11/20/14.

15   Ibid.

16   Ibid.

THE WISDOM LITERATURE

The books of Job, Psalms, Proverbs, and Ecclesiastes contain many nuggets of insight.

Job (Book of Job): The life of Job offers an incredible example of the sovereignty of God over our wealth—indeed, over our entire existence. A very wealthy man, Job was also incredibly righteous—"blameless and upright." Satan challenges God to allow Job's righteousness to be tested through the destruction of his household, the death of his children, the elimination of his wealth, and the loss of his health. Unaware of this wager between God and Satan, Job is forced to argue his innocence to his friends, who claim Job must have committed some grievous sin to deserve such punishment. In his defense, Job describes not only how he did not oppress the poor, but how he used his wealth to rescue and bless the needy. He "delivered" the poor and the fatherless; he caused the widow's heart to "sing for joy;" he was "eyes to the blind," "feet to the lame," and "father to the needy" (Job 29:12–17). He was even proactive, "search[ing] out the cause of him whom I did not know." (Job 29:16) Of course, Job also used his wealth to bless his family and community, regularly throwing feasts for his children and servants (Job 1:4-5). In chapter 31, Job articulates the appropriate attitude one should have toward wealth. Job "used [his wealth] generously, had not placed ultimate security in it, had [used it] in the service of others, and had not gained it through exploitation of his own employees."[17] From Job we learn how little control we have over our own wealth, as well as what responsible conduct looks like when we are blessed with wealth.

Psalms, Proverbs, and Ecclesiastes: This list is merely a scratch on the surface of the insight contained in these three great books.

---

17 Ibid.

Psalms

- Psalms 15 warns against seeking unfair financial gain.

- Psalms 37 reminds us that righteousness must be prioritized over wealth.

- Psalm 73 notes that life is often filled with economic injustice, which will only ultimately be resolved in eternity.

- Psalms 111 reiterates that all blessings come from the Lord.

- Psalms 112 articulates that we must be generous because of the Lord's generosity toward us.

Proverbs

- Proverbs 3:9–10 reminds us that God joyfully provides us with abundance.

- Proverbs 14:31 and 17:5 state that oppression of the poor is an "insult" to our Creator.

- Proverbs 19:17 states that generosity to the poor will be "repaid" by the Lord.

- Proverbs 22:2 reminds us that the poor and the rich are creatures of God alike.

- Proverbs 22:7 warns us that the borrower is a slave to his lender.

- Proverbs 23:4-5 warns against vain toiling to acquire wealth, for it "suddenly sprouts wings" and is gone.

- Proverbs 29:7 highlights that the righteous must affirm and defend the rights of the poor.

Ecclesiastes

- Ecclesiastes 2:9-11 describes how the author, King Solomon, had everything one could ever want, yet he ultimately concludes that "all was vanity and a striving after wind . . ."

- Ecclesiastes 5:10 cautions that "he who loves money will not be satisfied with money" because with a love of money comes excessive worry and fear.

- Ecclesiastes 5:19 counsels us to enjoy the blessings God gives us—indeed, He is the one who grants us the power to enjoy His provision.

- Ecclesiastes 9 reminds us that "man does not know his time [of death]," regardless of our worldly riches.

THE PROPHETS

Finally, we have the exhortations of the Prophets regarding how we should use our wealth. There are 17 books of Old Testament prophecy, which are replete with commentary on financial matters.

Most often, the prophets cry out against injustice, particularly injustice against the poor. Martin Luther King, Jr. famously quoted the prophet Amos when he declared: "Let justice roll down like waters!" (Amos 5:24). Amos chapter 8 contains a condemnation of those who cut corners or cheat to acquire more wealth in the marketplace.

Meanwhile, the prophet Isaiah decries those who fast for religious observance, while continuing to exploit the downtrodden. Through Isaiah, the Lord tells us that he would rather see us "loose the bonds of wickedness . . . to let the oppressed go free . . . to share your bread with the hungry and bring the homeless poor into your house" (Isaiah 58:6-7).

Micah calls Israel to a better way of living with the famous question, "What does the Lord require of you but to do justice, and to love kindness, and to walk humbly with your God?" (Micah 6:8).

Jeremiah condemns King Shallum, the son of righteous King Josiah, for pursuing a beautiful cedar home while failing to take up the cause of the impoverished. Jeremiah provocatively says that to judge fairly the cause of the poor and needy is to *know God* (Jeremiah 22:13-16).

In Habakkuk, we learn that we ought to rejoice in the God of our salvation, even when "the produce of the olive fails and the fields yield no food" (Habakkuk 3:17-19). Economic hardship should not cause us to stop relying upon or trusting in the Lord.

The Prophets present a stirring and convicting message about our wealth: that it ought to assist the cause of the needy, enact justice for the oppressed, and be gained through honest means, without exploiting the powerless.

Of course, God desires that we enjoy His tremendous provision, even as we simultaneously seek to serve others. In Malachi 3:10 we read, "Bring the full tithe into the storehouse, that there may be food in my house. And thereby put me to the test, says the Lord of hosts, if I will not open the windows of heaven for you and pour down for you a blessing until there is no more need."

OLD TESTAMENT CONCLUSIONS

What does the Old Testament teach us about wealth and giving? First, a proper use of one's possessions has been an important part of a right relationship with God since the very beginning. Righteousness is made visible through the generous and fair administration of wealth.

Second, for many biblical characters, faith played a major role in governing their behavior with regard to wealth and giving: positively for Abel, Abraham, Boaz, and Job; negatively for Cain and Jacob; and a mixed record for David and Solomon. The capacity of money to do much good, but also much harm, is likely why Scripture devotes so much space to the subject.

Third, God clearly considers enacting justice for the poor a key responsibility of those blessed with wealth—not by empty theologically "correct" words or affirmations, but through visible actions. Most importantly, we learn the appropriate relationship between ourselves, our wealth, and God. Deuteronomy 8:18 sums this up best: "You shall remember the Lord your God, for it is He who gives you power to get wealth . . ."

WEALTH AND GIVING IN THE NEW TESTAMENT

"For where your treasure is, there your heart will be also."
—Jesus, in Matthew 6:21

WHAT JESUS TAUGHT

Jesus spoke frequently on the topics of wealth, money, and giving. Here we explore a sample of His teachings selected to highlight the primary tenets of Jesus' view on these subjects.

Sermon on the Mount (Matthew 5-7; Luke 6): The Sermon on the Mount arguably took place relatively early in Jesus' ministry, soon after He had been baptized by John.[18] Jesus wasted no time in turning the world upside down with his teaching. In the Lukan version of the event, we read: "'Blessed are you who are poor, for yours is the kingdom of God. Blessed are you who hunger now, for you will be satisfied. . . . But woe to you who are rich, for

---

18 Deddo, Cathy. "Sermon on the Mount." http://www.trinitystudycenter.com/about_us.php. Accessed 3/23/15.

you have already received your comfort. Woe to you who are well fed now, for you will go hungry'" (Luke 6:20-21, 24-25). Some scholars call these verses the "Great Reversal" of Jesus' ministry—unlike traditional Jewish society, which elevated and honored the rich, Jesus came to support the poor and weak.[19, 20] Jesus' words are intended to highlight two important characteristics of God's Kingdom: the poor will finally be provided for as they seek God, while the rich must be wary of the tendency to delight in and trust their earthly riches instead of trusting in God. It is not poverty in itself that makes one blessed by God, but the humble, dependent, God-trusting disposition that we often find accompanying the oppressed poor in Scripture. Likewise, riches themselves are not wicked, but only if they are unrighteously obtained or used, a condition that is found only too frequently in this fallen world.

The Rich Young Ruler (Luke 18:18-30): A rich young man asks Jesus how he might obtain eternal life, pointing out that he has faithfully kept all the commandments (the Mosaic Law) his entire life. Jesus responds by instructing the young man to sell all his possessions, give them to the poor, and to come follow Him. Scripture tells us the rich man became "very sad," to which Jesus responds, "For it is easier for a camel to go through the eye of a needle than for a rich person to enter the Kingdom of God."

Many readers have questioned whether Jesus meant that all people must sell their possessions in order to follow Him, while others have wondered whether Jesus literally meant that no rich person could enter heaven. We do not believe this is the case.

First, in this very passage, Jesus qualifies his statement about excluding the rich, with these hopeful words, "What is impossible

---

19   Stanley, Brian. "Evangelical Social and Political Ethics: An Historical Perspective." Evangelical Quarterly 62.1 (1990), 19-36. Print.

20   Indeed, Jesus announces He had come to proclaim good news to the poor in Luke 4:18.

with man is possible with God" (verse 27).

Second, nowhere else in Scripture does Jesus command someone to sell all of his or her possessions, including other wealthy individuals with whom He interacts. For example, when the rich tax collector Zacchaeus gives away half his possessions in Luke 19, Jesus proclaims, "Today salvation has come to this house . . ." (Luke 19:9) That is, Jesus does not critically say, "Hey, you *only* gave away half!"

Many biblical scholars believe Jesus was stating that the rich man had made his wealth an idol. In Luke 16:13 Jesus states that, "no servant can serve two masters . . . You cannot serve God and money." In our view, this is the key point Jesus was making to the rich man: he could not follow Christ (and therefore obtain salvation) without renouncing his idolatry of his wealth by giving it away.

Parable of the Rich Fool (Luke 12:13-21): Jesus describes a rich man whose land "produced plentifully," completely filling up the man's barns. The man thought to himself, "I will tear down my barns and build larger ones, and there I will store all my grains and my goods. And I will say to my soul, 'Soul, you have ample goods laid up for many years; relax, eat, drink, and be merry.'" However, God says to him, "Fool! This night your soul is required of you, and the things you have prepared, whose will they be?" Jesus concludes, "So is the one who lays up treasure for himself and is not rich toward God." This parable starkly highlights the futility in accumulating wealth here on earth without a vision to use that wealth for eternal purposes. Not only are we wasting effort by accumulating assets that will soon fade away, but we are also deluding ourselves into thinking we have made ourselves secure. The reality is that we have placed our faith in "perishable goods!" This passage is particularly cutting for many Americans (ourselves included!) who aspire to build a "safe nest egg" for a 20+ year retirement.

The Rich Man and Lazarus (Luke 16:19-31): A rich man "was clothed in purple and fine linen and . . . feasted sumptuously every day," while at the rich man's gate laid "a poor man named Lazarus, covered with sores, who desired to be fed with what fell from the rich man's table." Both men die; the rich man finds himself in Hades, while Lazarus arrives by Abraham's side in heaven. The rich man calls out, "Father Abraham, have mercy on me, and send Lazarus to dip the end of his finger in water and cool my tongue, for I am in anguish in this flame." But Abraham denies the rich man's request, reminding the rich man that in life he "received [his] good things, and Lazarus in like manner bad things . . ."

The rich man did no direct harm to Lazarus while they were living. However, the rich man also did nothing to alleviate Lazarus' suffering, even as Lazarus laid at the rich man's gate begging for scraps every day. The rich man's first words to Abraham reveal his real problem: his callous heart toward Lazarus. Even from Hades, the rich man views Lazarus as inferior, as a task-boy. He does not even speak directly to Lazarus when asking for help! Had the rich man known and loved God, it would have shown in the way he treated those in need. The rich man's downfall was not his direct treatment of Lazarus, but rather his utter disregard for Lazarus, a fellow son of Abraham.

Store Up Treasure in Heaven (Luke 12:33-34): The previous four passages highlight the futility—the spiritual danger, even— of accumulating and trusting in wealth. So what should we do with our wealth? Jesus says in this passage, "Sell your possessions and give to the needy. Provide yourselves with moneybags that do not grow old, with a treasure in heaven that does not fail, where no thief approaches and no moth destroys. For where your treasure is, there your heart will be also." Christian economist and author Ron McKenzie sums up this passage up well: "The best way to shift wealth to heaven is to give to the poor."[21]

Rather than accumulating wealth in this world, we should accumulate "wealth" in heaven by doing God's work here on earth. Jesus' message goes much deeper than simply transferring "assets" to a safer "bank," however. Jesus' words offer a sharp insight into sinful human nature: we are naturally wired to focus on hoarding wealth and are prone to narcissistic consumption. To the extent we focus on our earthly treasure, we run the risk of becoming corrupted by materialism, selfishness, and greed. Conversely, focusing on our heavenly treasure enables us to experience God's holy blessings of selflessness, service, and peace.

The Final Judgment (Matthew 25:31-45): The final teaching of Jesus we explore paints a bold picture of God's intentions for our wealth. Jesus' words are too powerful to summarize, so we quote the passage in full:

> "When the Son of Man comes in his glory, and all the angels with him, then he will sit on his glorious throne. Before him will be gathered all the nations, and he will separate people one from another as a shepherd separates the sheep from the goats. And he will place the sheep on his right, but the goats on the left. Then the King will say to those on his right, 'Come, you who are blessed by my Father, inherit the kingdom prepared for you from the foundation of the world. For I was hungry and you gave me food, I was thirsty and you gave me drink, I was a stranger and you welcomed me, I was naked and you clothed me, I was sick and you visited me, I was

---

21 McKenzie, Ron. "Jesus on Money." http://kingwatch.co.nz/Christian_Political_Economy/jesus_on_money.htm. Accessed 11/20/14.

in prison and you came to me.' Then the righteous will answer him, saying, 'Lord, when did we see you hungry and feed you, or thirsty and give you drink? And when did we see you a stranger and welcome you, or naked and clothe you? And when did we see you sick or in prison and visit you?' And the King will answer them, 'Truly, I say to you, as you did it to one of the least of these my brothers, you did it to me.'

"Then he will say to those on his left, 'Depart from me, you cursed, into the eternal fire prepared for the devil and his angels. For I was hungry and you gave me no food, I was thirsty and you gave me no drink, I was a stranger and you did not welcome me, naked and you did not clothe me, sick and in prison and you did not visit me.' Then they also will answer, saying, 'Lord, when did we see you hungry or thirsty or a stranger or naked or sick or in prison, and did not minister to you?' Then he will answer them, saying, 'Truly, I say to you, as you did not do it to one of the least of these, you did not do it to me.'"

Jesus uses very clear language regarding what we as Christians are called to do with our wealth: serve the poor. Indeed, Jesus goes so far as to state that by serving the poor, we are serving Him *directly*. (This is reminiscent of Jeremiah's claim that to care for the cause of the needy is to *know God*.) It is likely that in this parable, Jesus is specifically focusing God's broad concern for the destitute more narrowly on Christians, or Christian messengers, in poverty. (Note Jesus' explicit language, "the least of these my brothers.") Indeed, if we do not care practically for the pressing needs of those in our "spiritual family," our supposed relationship with that family is called into question. That seems to be Jesus' main point. The way we treat other Christians in need really shows who we are—and our deeds will testify to that truth on the Day of Judgment.

In speaking about care for other believers, Jesus does not deny our broader obligation to care for any person in need. We are reminded of Paul's similar exhortation in Galatians 6:10: "Therefore, as we have opportunity, let us do good to all people, *especially to those who belong to the family of believers,*" (emphasis added).

How might we summarize Jesus' teaching on wealth and giving? The "Great Reversal" articulated by Jesus during the Sermon on the Mount highlights both God's love for the poor and the natural tendency of the rich to become overly reliant on their wealth. The Rich Young Ruler and the Parable of the Rich Fool underscore the danger and futility of idolizing and accumulating wealth. The Parable of the Rich Man and Lazarus highlights the sin in ignoring the poor; rather, we must show regard for them and proactively meet their needs. The command to store up treasure in heaven offers important insight into how dangerous and seductive an idol wealth really is. Finally, the Final Judgment, offered near the end of Jesus' ministry, comes full circle with the Sermon on the Mount: Jesus so closely identifies with the poor that He states we are serving Him directly when we serve them. Jesus' lessons on wealth and money are hard, but they are clear. He has high expectations for how we manage our wealth and giving.

WHAT THE APOSTLES TAUGHT

We now move into the back half of the New Testament, summarizing what the apostles and other New Testament writers have to say about wealth, money, and giving. Unsurprisingly, the apostles and other New Testament writers align closely with the teachings of Jesus on these subjects. Again, we have selected but a few of the many New Testament passages related to these topics. We group the passages into two core themes: our attitude toward wealth and money, and our attitude toward giving.

Attitude Toward Wealth and Money: The writer of Hebrews cautions us to "keep your life free from the love of money, and be content with what you have . . ." (Hebrews 13:5). Paul reaffirms Jesus' teaching when he says, " . . . we brought nothing into this world, and we cannot take anything out of this world. . . . But those who desire to be rich fall into temptation, into a snare, into many senseless and harmful desires that plunge people into ruin and destruction. For the love of money is the root of all kinds of evil" (1 Timothy 6:7, 9-10). Note that Paul does not say that *money* is the root of all kinds of evil, but rather *the love of money*. He goes on to provide wise counsel to the rich "in this present age," " . . . charge them not to be haughty, nor to set their hopes on the uncertainty of riches, but on God, who richly provides us with everything to enjoy. They are to do good, to be rich in good works, to be generous and ready to share, thus storing up treasure for themselves as a good foundation for the future, so that they may take hold of that which is truly life" (1 Timothy 6:17-19).

Attitude Toward Giving: Luke says, "In all things I have shown you that by working hard in this way we must help the weak and remember the words of the Lord Jesus, how He Himself said, 'It is more blessed to give than to receive'" (Acts 20:35).

Of course, one way we give is by providing for our family. Paul states, "But if anyone does not provide for his relatives, and especially for his own household, he has denied the faith and is worse than an unbeliever."[22] Paul also elaborates on the appropriate attitude,

---

22 1 Timothy 5:8. Note that Paul states, "does not provide for his relatives…" rather than "cannot provide for his relatives…" Deuteronomy 15:11 states that "There will always be poor people in the land…" It is not a sin to be unable to provide for one's family, so long as one genuinely attempts to do so. Here, Paul is strictly speaking of individuals who could provide for their families but elect not to, due to selfishness or poor financial decision making.

amount, motivation, and usage for giving. He writes, "But as you excel in everything . . . see that you excel in this act of grace [i.e., giving] also . . . Your abundance at the present time should supply their need, so that their abundance may supply your need . . .Each one must give as he has decided in his heart, not reluctantly or under compulsion, for God loves a cheerful giver . . . You will be enriched in every way to be generous in every way, which through us will produce thanksgiving to God" (2 Corinthians 8:7, 14; 9:7, 11).

These passages by Paul and other New Testament writers affirm Jesus' teachings on wealth and money by highlighting the temptation and futility of pursuing wealth, encouraging us to store up treasure in heaven, and reiterating the importance of giving generously to the poor.

A BRIEF NOTE ON TITHING IN THE NEW COVENANT

"With the price of everything else going up these days, aren't you glad the Lord hasn't increased the tithe to 15 percent?"
—Anonymous

We want to briefly discuss a contentious topic in the Church today: are Christians required to tithe? Here we specifically define tithing as a religious contribution equal to 10 percent of one's income. Teaching on tithing today can be broadly bucketed into three categories:

1. Christians are required to tithe;

2. Christians "should" tithe, even if we are not technically required to do so; and

3. Christians are not required to tithe.

Even pastors are split on the subject. In 2011, a survey of pastors and leaders of denominations was conducted by the National Association of Evangelicals, mission organizations, and Christian universities. The survey found that 42 percent of respondents believe that giving 10 percent of one's income is mandated of New Covenant believers by the Bible, while 58 percent do not.[23]

Why the split opinion? Commenting on the NAE survey, Dr. John Walton, Professor of Old Testament at Wheaton College, said it all goes "back to the old argument—are we under law or under grace?"[24] That is to say, to what extent were the Old Testament laws abrogated (i.e., fulfilled and therefore no longer required) by Christ's death? Jesus says, "Do not think I have come to abolish the Law or the Prophets; I have not come to abolish them but to fulfill them" (Matthew 5:17). However, the apostle Paul says, " . . . you are not under law but under grace," (Romans 6:14) and continues, "For Christ is the end of the law for righteousness to everyone who believes" (Romans 10:4).

A common way of explaining this apparent discrepancy is that Christ fulfilled the civil and ceremonial aspects of the Old Testament law. (Thus believers do not offer temple sacrifices, and they eat pork.) Christ also fulfilled the moral requirements of the law through his perfectly obedient life and his death for our moral failure. Yet, in so far as the commands in the Old Testament reflect timeless moral truth (grounded in the very nature of God and structure of creation), they continue to find expression in the Spirit-empowered obedience of God's New Covenant people.

The question, then, is which Old Testament commands represent an inherent moral principle and should therefore be upheld today

---

23 Vu, Michelle. "Most Evangelical Leaders Say Tithe Not Required by Bible." Published in Christian Post. 4/7/11. http://www.christianpost.com/news/most-evangelical-leaders-say-tithe-not-required-by-bible-49744/. Accessed 11/21/14.

24 Ibid.

(e.g., "Thou shalt not kill"), versus which Old Testament commands are civil, ceremonial, or culturally conditioned in some way? Bible-believing Christians sometimes disagree on these issues.

We both grew up in typical conservative evangelical churches where the tithe was the gold standard, at least in practice if not in rule. However, after researching the subject for ourselves, we have come to the view that Christians are not required to tithe.[25] We hold this view for several reasons. First, the Mosaic Law actually commanded three distinct tithes—the Levitical Tithe, the Festival Tithe, and the Charity Tithe. When added together, these three tithes represented approximately 23 percent of an Israelite's income every year. To the extent Christians are using the Old Testament law as the basis for requiring a tithe today, it should be 23 percent, not 10 percent![26] (Of course, if we follow the Old Testament tithe laws exactly, part of those tithes should be employed to fund a trip and throw a celebration!)

Second, neither Jesus, Paul, nor any of the other New Testament writers specifically command Christians to tithe. Jesus only explicitly mentions tithing twice: Matthew 23:23 and Luke 18:9-14.[27] In Matthew 23 Jesus admonishes the Pharisees for succumbing to legalism by tithing their homegrown herbs and spices while neglecting "weightier matters" like justice, mercy, and faithfulness. In Luke 18, Jesus tells a parable contrasting a proud Pharisee with a repentant tax collector, again warning us against legalism and reminding us to remain humble in our faith. The main point Jesus is making in both of these passages is not related

---

25 We make frequent use of Professor David Croteau's excellent work *You Mean I Don't Have to Tithe?* in this section.

26 It should be noted that freewill offerings (i.e., giving above the required tithe) did in fact exist in the Old Testament as well (Exodus 35:29; Deuteronomy 16:10; Ezra 3:5, etc.). Thus, the argument that New Covenant believers are required to give freewill offerings instead of an Old Testament tithe is invalid, or at least incomplete.

27 Jesus' words in Matthew 23:23 are also paraphrased in Luke 11:42.

to tithing; rather, Jesus is making a separate point, with tithing serving as a "prop" of sorts to support his argument.[28]

The New Testament includes other passages where Jesus, Paul, or other writers do not directly mention tithing, but may discuss the "concept" of tithing.[29] Of these, the most interesting are Matthew 22:15-22 ("Give to Caesar what is Caesar's and give to God what is God's") and 1 Corinthians 9:13-14 (" . . . the Lord commanded that those who proclaim the gospel should get their living by the gospel"). Again, neither passage is about tithing *per se* (i.e., neither Jesus' nor Paul's primary points were related to tithing) and, in our view, neither passage is strong enough to affirmatively institute tithing as a command in the New Covenant.[30]

Finally, the New Testament offers a great deal of instruction on giving. The core message of this instruction is that rather than following a strict formula, Christian giving should exhibit a set of qualitative traits which honor and reflect God's character.

- Second Corinthians 8:3 and 9:7 teach that giving should be of free volition (i.e., not compulsory).

- Second Corinthians 8:2-3 and Philippians 4:17-18 teach that giving should be generous; Mark 12:42-44 goes further, teaching that God honors sacrificial giving.

- Second Corinthians 9:7 teaches that we should give cheerfully.

- Second Corinthians 8:4-5 and 1 Corinthians 9:3-14 teach that giving should support local ministers.

---

28 Croteau, *You Mean I Don't Have to Tithe?*, 131.

29 Matthew 22:15-22; 1 Corinthians 9:13-14; 16:1-4; 2 Corinthians 8:8; 9:7; Galatians 6:6

30 Croteau, *You Mean I Don't Have to Tithe?*, 137.

- Acts 20:35 and Matthew 25:31-45, among many other passages, state that giving must support the poor and needy in our communities.

These traits of our giving—voluntary, generous (even sacrificial), cheerful, and supportive of local ministers and the poor—all reflect God Himself in His generous giving (James 1:17-18). Rather than following strict laws, the mode of giving outlined in the New Testament actually frees Christians to generously serve others out of thankfulness to God for His provision.

All that said, we do believe both tithing itself and the teaching of tithing in churches offer several practical benefits, even if it is not explicitly required of New Covenant believers. In his excellent book, *Money, Possessions, and Eternity*, Randy Alcorn calls tithing "the training wheels of giving."[31] He offers several specific benefits of tithing, including the ease with which it can be taught to others (especially children), its clarity and sharpness as a spiritual discipline, its demonstrated force as a catalyst of overall spiritual growth, and its effectiveness as a starting point for learning the joy of giving.[32]

We also believe there is psychological benefit in adopting a "first fruits" mentality with respect to our income. In the Pentateuch, God commanded the Israelites to offer to Him the first 10 percent of nearly everything they produced.[33] Alcorn states that by giving the *first* 10 percent, the Israelites were making a clear statement: "We give of our first and best to you, Lord, because we recognize all good things come from you."[34] Tithing our "first" 10 percent of income can help us make this same statement today as well.

---

31 Alcorn, *Money, Possessions, and Eternity*, 174.

32 Ibid., 182-185.

33 This included wine in Leviticus 19:23-25, agricultural products in Exodus 23:16, Exodus 34:22, and Deuteronomy 18:4, and livestock in Exodus 34:19.

34 Ibid., 175.

Ultimately, our view is that tithing is not a requirement, but can be an excellent starting point for Christians seeking to honor God through their generosity. We agree with Alcorn that Jesus "never lowered the bar. He always raised it."[35] Recall what Jesus says about murder, adultery, and following through on promises in Matthew 5:17-48. We believe the same is true of tithing. Our ambition is to strive for a level of generosity far exceeding the Old Testament tithe.[36]

THE POWER OF THE BIBLE'S TEACHING ON WEALTH AND GIVING

Hebrews 4:12 says that God's Word is "living and active . . . piercing to the division of soul and spirit . . . discerning the thoughts and intentions of the heart." The power of the Bible's teaching on wealth and giving extends far beyond a mere intellectual investigation: it has the power to change hearts, the power to save souls. During our research we met a man who knows the power of God's teaching on wealth and giving firsthand. Brandon Fremont speaks with the smooth, distinctive accent unique to those who grew up in the southern bayous of Louisiana. He also speaks with a level of confidence and conviction that only comes from a deep understanding of who you are and what your role is on this earth. Now in his early forties, Brandon is a partner at a successful hedge fund in Chicago, Illinois. Around 15 years ago, his wife and some close friends asked if Brandon would read the Bible with them and meet weekly to discuss what they had read. Brandon agreed; over a period of 15 months he read the entire Bible—from Genesis to

---

35 Ibid., 182.

36 This view is bolstered by the fact that all of us are much wealthier than the Israelites were. According to Eric Beinhocker's *The Origins of Wealth*, GDP (Gross Domestic Product) per capita in the ancient Mediterranean was roughly $150. If we generously assume each person in a family received this amount, a family of four would live on approximately $600 per year! If God's Law asked for generous gifts from those earning a $600 annual income, what might it ask of a society blessed with median family earnings of over $50,000, or roughly 85 times higher?

Revelation—and gave his heart to Christ in the process. Brandon says, "God revealed His story of grace to me, and my life was changed forever."

Given his role as a professional money manager, wealth was one area in which Brandon was excited to apply his new faith. "I was growing in my walk with Christ during this time. Giving was one avenue where I was excited to grow as a Christ-follower. I picked a few topics and said, 'I want to understand everything Scripture says about this topic.'" Brandon spent hours studying the Bible's teaching on money, and also credits Randy Alcorn's *Money, Possessions, and Eternity* as a significant influence.

"I came away thinking the tithe is a minimum, a starting point. My wife and I were at a church at the time that did annual commitments—where you pledged how much you would give for the entire year. I arrived at church for annual Commitment Day. We were ready to pledge 10 percent. They showed the number of people in different buckets [by amount given]. I did some quick math—at 10 percent, we were going to be in top one percent of the church! The pastor stood up that day and said, 'I'm not going to ask people to tithe—I don't think that's realistic. But I am going to ask people to give more than they gave last year.'"

Considering the relative affluence of his church, Brandon figured he'd be in the little leagues with a 10 percent giving commitment. But the data showed he'd be in the top one percent of his church! And the pastor was okay with this! Brandon laments, "That [Commitment Sunday] was really sad. That month was the first time I really wrestled through the issue of giving."

Despite this setback, Brandon continued to honor his understanding of God's teaching on wealth. "Over the following years my income increased every year. We would give disproportionately more of [our incremental income] to God every year. The question I always asked myself was, 'What am I doing with that *more?*' After three or four years, we were giving 100 percent of our incremental income over the prior year."

By the time Brandon made partner, he was giving 40 to 60 percent of his total income to God each year. But he is quick to note that stewardship is not just about giving as much as possible. "Faithfulness is what matters. You don't want to give a ton, but not think about your other spending decisions. And you don't want to just cut a 10-percent check and then do whatever you want with the rest of your money. Rather than looking at it through spreadsheets or drawing a line in the sand, I ask myself, 'Do I feel good about [my faithfulness in] everything I'm doing?' Let's always go back to being biblical—what does Scripture say about this? I ask myself, 'What is Godly wisdom on this decision? OK, let's do that.' I'm a steward in the mystery of Christ—I'm just going to reflect Scripture." Brandon calls it being "on mission" for Christ.

In addition to giving generously, Brandon also co-authored a small group curriculum for his church designed to teach others how to steward wealth and money in a God-honoring way. The first ground rule listed on the first page of the study states, "Focus on God's Word regarding the subject . . ."

We will return to Brandon's story later. For now, notice how his story began in the first place: by digging deeply into God's Word, especially God's teaching about wealth and giving. God's Word transformed Brandon's life, unlocking an incredible spirit of generosity inside him.

Scripture includes over 2,000 verses on wealth and money for a reason: our handling of wealth is critical to our relationship with God! Randy Alcorn said it best: "God sees our finances and our faith as inseparable."[37] As Christ followers, we must thoughtfully examine all God has to say on the subject. When I (Greg) did so, I was blown away by the consistency, clarity, and force of God's message. His teaching is hard, but only by embracing that teaching will we learn to experience the unique, life-giving joy God offers to those who live generously.

37 Alcorn, *The Treasure Principle*, 8.

CHAPTER TWO

Seven Core Principles for Biblical Wealth and Giving

"Everything we have is a gift from God, including wealth. Yet as I watch myself and other Christians gain greater income and wealth, I see the profound truth in biblical warnings about wealth being a snare and the love of money (which can crop up any time) becoming the root of all kinds of evil. Sadly, it's true."

—Response to survey of Christian business leaders we conducted as part of Harvard Divinity School course

Before we jump into this chapter, we want to first acknowledge the many, many scholars who have come before us in studying money and its relationship to Scripture. We have included a reading list in the appendix and highly recommend each resource to anyone who is interested in learning more about how to honor God with our money.

We began this project by conducting a longitudinal study of Scripture on the subject of wealth and giving. Through this study, we learned so much about the consistency, clarity, and force of God's teaching on the subject. However, we were struggling to translate all of that biblical knowledge into a pragmatic framework for managing our own wealth. We needed a bridge between the wisdom of the patriarchs, prophets, and Jesus, and the answer to real-life questions like, "How should I think about buying a house?"

It seemed like we were new employees on an oil rig who had read the company's 2,000-page safe practices manual, but weren't sure how to actually begin working. We needed a wallet-sized, laminated "Top Safety Tenets" card with the primary safety instructions needed to prevent newbies like us from experiencing serious injury or death while on site.

Every verse of God's teaching on money is full of wisdom and insight. However, sometimes we humans need a "summary version" to help us apply those teachings to our everyday lives. So we spent a long time attempting to distill down all 2,350 Bible verses on money into a "Top Wealth and Giving Tenets" card. This chapter presents what we're calling the Seven Core Principles of Biblical Wealth and Giving. Think of these core principles as tools for translating God's lessons on money into our modern-day, daily decision making on wealth and giving.

To be clear, we are simply restating what God has already said. The seven principles that follow are our attempt to summarize God's teaching on money, wealth, and giving, while adding nothing of our own. While we hope the prior chapter presented a compelling overview of God's teaching on money, we also recommend that every Christian conduct his or her own longitudinal study of Scripture on the subject. Were you to do so, you may decide there are actually six or eight core principles—not seven. That's fine. We are not arguing that our seven principles somehow carry God's holy stamp of approval. For us, they are simply a useful tool for ensuring that our framework for managing our own wealth and giving is both firmly founded in God's teaching and practical for making real-life financial decisions.

All that said, after going through this exercise, we do think we stumbled upon one new and useful insight—well, at least it was new and useful for us! Throughout our research we had been pursuing the question of how to manage our wealth in a Godly way, with a specific focus on how much we should give. It finally dawned on us that we were thinking about the question backward. A faithful reading of Scripture leads not to the question, "How much should I give?" Rather, it leads to the question, "How much do I need to keep?"

This new insight hit us like a brick after debating and forming the core principles for an extended period of time. We have come to view this insight as the natural conclusion of biblical teaching on money. We make the case for the validity of this insight—it's not "How much should I give?" but rather "How much do I need to keep?"—through the Seven Core Principles of Biblical Wealth and Giving.

Table 1: Seven Core Principles for Biblical Wealth and Giving

Category	Principle
Wealth	1. Everything we "own" actually belongs to God. *Everything.*
	2. "Our" wealth and possessions should be used for God's purposes.
	3. Wealth is like dynamite, with great potential for both good and harm.
	4. Worldly wealth is fleeting; heavenly treasure is eternal.
Giving	5. Giving generously to the poor is a moral duty in a fallen world.
	6. Giving should be voluntary, generous (even sacrificial), cheerful, and needs-based.
	7. Giving generously breaks the power of money over us.

PRINCIPLE ONE: EVERYTHING WE OWN BELONGS TO GOD. *EVERYTHING.*

An appropriate understanding of wealth and giving begins with the recognition that everything we own actually belongs to God. However, actually embracing this attitude is incredibly difficult. While many of us are willing to acknowledge God's sovereignty over natural creation—mountains, oceans, even the blessing of human life—we are typically loath to attribute similar sovereignty over our houses, vacation plans, and paychecks.

One possible reason for this is humans' natural tendency to attribute our successes to internal factors but to attribute our failures to external factors.[38] In other words, we naturally over-emphasize our own role when good things happen in our lives.

---

38   Forsyth, Donelson: "Self-Serving Bias." https://facultystaff.richmond.edu/~dforsyth/pubs/forsyth2008selfserving.pdf. Accessed 11/18/14.

Even when we do give God credit, we often see Him as part of our supporting cast, while we maintain the lead role. "Thanks be to God for putting me in the position to earn this promotion—all my hard work finally paid off!"

In contrast, a proper understanding of our possessions—indeed, our entire existence—is through the lens of God's sovereignty. All things were created by Him and for Him (Colossians 1:16). Therefore, all things belong to Him (1 Chronicles 29:11). This includes ourselves: "You are not your own, for you were bought with a price" (1 Corinthians 6:19-20). Unfortunately, we often fail to recognize this fact. A friend of ours quipped, "We are living sacrifices, but unfortunately we often climb off the altar!"

Even when we "earn" something (e.g., when we work hard to save money for a down payment on a house) we do so by using skills given to us by God (Psalms 144:1), in a job gifted to us by God (Exodus 20:9), with the support of an organization and a political economy that are both ordained by God (Romans 13:1-2), all of which are held in existence moment-by-moment through God (Colossians 1:17). In other words, the credit is all His. What are the implications of this? First, we should be overwhelmed with gratitude toward God for His abundant blessing. Second, we should recognize the importance of our role as stewards of God's possessions.

PRINCIPLE TWO: OUR WEALTH AND POSSESSIONS SHOULD BE USED FOR GOD'S PURPOSES.

Scripture is clear that God has called us to be stewards of His possessions (Luke 12:42-43). However, we believe there is a fundamental misunderstanding in the church today around the notion of stewardship. The term "stewardship" has been watered down by countless "Stewardship Committees," "Stewardship Sundays," and "Annual Stewardship Drives." In many churches, "stewardship" has essentially become synonymous with "writing a check to the church once a month." We would like to elevate the term back to its original meaning with the following definition:

> *Stewardship is the active and responsible management of God's creation for God's purposes.*

The key distinction in this revised definition is an impetus for *action*. Stewardship requires that we actively engage in the utilization and distribution of God's resources to accomplish His objectives. This includes giving, but also entails so much more: praying for wisdom in allocating His resources; providing leadership to organizations (church or para-church) that are utilizing or distributing those resources; and directly utilizing or distributing those resources ourselves. A steward is not just responsible for collecting and distributing funds; he is also responsible for how those funds are used—indeed, for the actual outcomes obtained through the use of those resources.

Note that this definition of stewardship applies to *all* our resources, not just our tithes and offerings. If we embrace this definition, all of our purchases should be made through the lens of furthering God's Kingdom. The resources we spend on our family, leisure, and entertainment should be seen as a means to serve God's Kingdom: our homes always open to guests, our car keys held out in open hands, our fridges free to be raided.

At the same time, it would be a mistake to conclude that simply spending less is the primary directive of stewardship. Paul says we ought to "set [our] hopes on . . . God, who richly provides us everything to enjoy" (1 Timothy 6:17). The Psalmist concurs: "You shall eat the fruit of your labor of your hands; you shall be blessed, and it shall be well with you" (Psalms 128:2). While God's purposes certainly include delivering justice to the underprivileged, His purposes also include our enjoyment of His blessings. Both purposes are legitimate.

We must be active, thoughtful, strategic stewards of God's possessions. Sometimes that means giving sacrificially back to the Lord. Other times, that means spending quality time with your family at the beach! The point is to have a clear picture of *why* you're using God's resources in the ways you choose—to be certain you can "offer up this purchase as a sacrifice to the Lord."[39]

PRINCIPLE THREE: WEALTH IS LIKE DYNAMITE, WITH GREAT POTENTIAL FOR BOTH GOOD AND HARM.[40]

Money is one of the strongest forces on the planet. Author and poet Carl Sandburg said that "Money is power, freedom, a cushion, the root of all evil, the sum of blessings."[41] Money itself is not inherently good or bad, but it is powerful. Further, humans are particularly susceptible to the temptation to fall in love with money, and our character is incredibly vulnerable to its corrosive influence. John Steinbeck wrote, "A strange species we are. We can stand anything God and nature can throw at us save only plenty."[42] Proverbs 30 echoes similar sentiments: "Give me neither poverty nor riches; feed me with the food that I need, or I shall be full, and deny you, and say, 'Who is the Lord?' or I shall be poor, and steal, and profane the name of my God."

---

39 Fremont, Brandon. Author interview. February 18, 2015.

40 We are grateful to Will Messenger and the Theology of Work project for first articulating the analogy of money as a stick of dynamite.

41 Sandburg, Carl. As quoted by Jackson, Keith in "The Last Word on Money." http://www.independent.co.uk/news/business/the-last-word-on-money-1574900.html. Accessed 3/19/15.

42 John Steinbeck, as quoted in Alcorn, *Money, Possessions, and Eternity*, 46.

Paul Piff, a psychologist and professor at University of California, Irvine, studies how money influences humans' relationships with one another and has seen this corrosive influence in action. His striking conclusion is that money makes us mean. Piff describes one of his experiments involving two individuals playing a rigged game of Monopoly.

> *We . . . randomly assigned one of the two [players] to be a rich player in a rigged game [of Monopoly]. They got two times as much money. When they passed "GO," they collected twice the salary, and they got to roll both dice instead of one . . . It was quickly apparent to players that . . . one person clearly has more money than the other. As the game unfolded, we saw very dramatic differences emerge . . . The rich player started to move around the board louder, literally smacking the board with their piece . . . we were more likely to see signs of dominance, displays of power and celebration among the rich players. The rich players actually started to become ruder toward the other person, less and less sensitive, and more and more demonstrative of their materials success.*
>
> *Quotes from rich players [include]: "I have money for everything . . . you're going to lose all your money soon . . . I have so much money, I'm going to buy out this whole board . . . I'm pretty much untouchable at this point . . ."*
>
> *When the rich players talked [afterward] about why they had (inevitably) won in this rigged game, they talked about what they'd done to buy those different*

properties and earn their success . . . That's a really incredible insight into how the mind makes sense of advantage.[43]

Piff has conducted similar experiments with real-life wealthy individuals and discovered identical results. His experiments have tested individuals' willingness to stop for pedestrians at crosswalks, cheat in a computer game, share a monetary gift with strangers, and even take candy from a jar clearly labeled as being for children. In *every experiment*, higher incomes were correlated with "mean" behavior![44] Piff elaborates, "What we've been finding . . . is that as a person's level of wealth increases, their feelings of compassion and empathy go down, and their feelings of entitlement, of deservingness, and their ideology of self-interest increase."[45]

It turns out that just feeling wealthy—even with fake money in a rigged game!—can easily turn us into awful human beings. No wonder God so strongly warns us of the corrosive power of wealth.[46] Piff's research lends additional weight to Jesus' claim that "where your treasure is, there will your heart be also" (Luke 12:34). We must always be vigilant to harness the power of money for God's glory, while simultaneously protecting ourselves from its potentially corruptive and divisive influence in our lives.

---

43 Piff, Paul. December 2013. Paul Piff: *Does Money Make You Mean?* [Video File]. Retrieved from http://www.ted.com/talks/paul_piff_does_money_make_you_mean/transcript?language=en. Accessed 3/9/15.

44 Ibid.

45 Ibid.

46 1 Timothy 6:10; James 5:1-5

PRINCIPLE FOUR: WORLDLY WEALTH IS FLEETING; HEAVENLY TREASURE IS ETERNAL.

Randy Alcorn offers the following illustration in his outstanding book *The Treasure Principle*:

> *Imagine you're alive at the end of the Civil War. You're living in the South, but you are a Northerner. You plan to move home as soon as the war is over. While in the South you've accumulated lots of Confederate currency. Now, suppose you know for a fact that the North is going to win the war and the end is imminent. What will you do with your Confederate money?*
>
> *If you're smart, there's only one answer. You should immediately cash in your Confederate currency for U.S. Currency—the only money that will have value once the war is over. Keep only enough Confederate currency to meet your short-term needs.*[47]

Alcorn's point is clear. As Christians, we have inside knowledge of the final outcome—of the coming of God's Kingdom.[48] Therefore, accumulating vast earthly treasure we cannot possibly use is short-sighted at best, if not a complete waste of time. As we all know, "there are no pockets in a shroud and no U-Hauls behind a hearse."[49]

---

47 Alcorn, Randy. *The Treasure Principle*, 14.

48 Alcorn wittily calls this the "ultimate insider trading tip."

49 Anonymous quote we discovered during our research.

Jesus went so far as to call the rich man storing up his wealth here on earth a "fool" (Luke 12: 13-21). Instead, we must focus on storing up treasure in heaven. This means maintaining an "eternal perspective" when managing our wealth. The prophet Isaiah exhorts us, "Why do you spend your money on that which is not bread, and your labor for that which does not satisfy?" (Isaiah 55:2) When deciding how to manage our giving, consumption, and savings (all are important!), we must ask ourselves which course of action will most glorify God and most benefit His Kingdom on Earth. A proper attitude toward wealth prioritizes treasure in heaven over treasure on Earth. As Christians, we recognize that we must temporarily use Earth's currency. We just need to remember it is temporary when we decide how to use it!

An acute danger of our incredible wealth today is that we can frequently give an amount that "sounds" generous, but in fact costs us very little. We think we can "eat, drink, and be merry" now, while simultaneously socking away enough treasure in heaven to live the good life once we get there, too. Unfortunately, owning two separate treasure troves isn't an option: immediately after calling the rich man storing up his worldly wealth a fool, Jesus adds, "So is the one who lays up treasure for himself and is not rich toward God."[50]

What value will our "Confederate" houses, cars, wardrobes, and retirement accounts have when we meet Jesus? God can produce blessing out of any amount we invest in His Kingdom. But He also evaluates the amount we choose to invest in *our own* kingdoms. God desires for us to enjoy His blessings, but to do so through the lens of His eternal Kingdom, not our own temporary one. We must be thoughtful about where we choose to store our treasure.

---

50 Luke 12:21; to be fair, many Proverbs speak about wise planning for the future. But, there is a difference between wise planning and hoarding.

PRINCIPLE FIVE: GIVING GENEROUSLY TO THE POOR IS A MORAL DUTY IN A FALLEN WORLD.

We live in a fallen world, a consequence of which is the existence of human suffering. The Theology of Work Project reports that 1.4 billion people live in extreme poverty, meaning they lack the resources for basic provision. A further 1.1 billion people live at subsistence level, "on a kind of hand-to-mouth existence."[51] These statistics imply more than one of every three humans alive today lives in poverty.

Nowhere does God promise material abundance for all mankind; indeed, Scripture indicates that this life will be difficult for many followers of God.[52] The ancient Israelites were told that "there will always be poor people in the land . . ." (Deuteronomy 15:11). However, God has a deep and profound love for all His creation.[53] And based on the teachings of Jesus we explored in Chapter One, God has a particularly strong affiliation with the poor. Therefore, we as the Church have a moral obligation to support our fellow man, especially the poor. Pope Francis stated this well when he wrote that the Church should have a "preferential option for the poor."[54]

Arthur Simon, former President of Bread for the World, notes that "there is a connection between empty stomachs on one continent

---

51 Kirkland, Wayne. "Provision and Wealth Overview," The Theology of Work Project, 3.

52 Genesis 3:17; Psalms 60:1-3

53 John 3:16; Romans 5:8

54 Pope Francis. *The Joy of the Gospel*, 158. For purposes of clarity, we agree with Pope Francis' statement in the sense of James 2:5 ("Listen, my beloved brothers, has not God chosen those who are poor in the world to be rich in faith and heirs of the kingdom, which He has promised to those who love Him?"). However, unlike some in the liberation theology movement, we do not believe poverty is inherently valued by God, regardless of one's disposition toward God.

and empty lives on another."[55] Failing to support the poor is a sign we do not "know" God—that we do not understand either His love for His creation or our role in implementing His purposes on Earth. Now that we serve as Jesus' hands and feet, we must take up the mantle from Jesus in caring for the disenfranchised (Romans 12:3-8). Saint Teresa of Avila, a 16th-century nun and author, wrote the following poem entitled "Christ Has No Body." If Christ's followers don't care for those whom He loves, who will?

> *Christ has no body but yours,*
> *No hands, no feet on earth but yours,*
> *Yours are the eyes with which He looks,*
> *Compassion on this world,*
> *Yours are the feet with which He walks to do good,*
> *Yours are the hands with which He blesses all the world.*
> *Yours are the hands, yours are the feet,*
> *Yours are the eyes, you are His body.*
> *Christ has no body now but yours,*
> *No hands, no feet on earth but yours,*
> *Yours are the eyes with which He looks*
> *Compassion on this world,*
> *Christ has no body now on earth but yours.*[56]

Our moral duty to support the poor is reinforced by the fact that today, perhaps for the first time in history, humankind collectively has access to sufficient resources to provide basic provision to all people. English novelist John Berger says, "The poverty of our century is unlike that of any other. It is not, as poverty was before, the result of natural scarcity, but of a set of priorities imposed upon the rest of the world by the rich. Consequently, the modern poor

---

55 Simon, Arthur. *How Much is Enough?*, 18.

56 Avila, Teresa. "Christ Has No Body." http://www.journeywithjesus.net/PoemsAndPrayers/Teresa_Of_Avila_Christ_Has_No_Body.shtml. Accessed 3/10/15.

are not pitied . . . but written-off as trash. The twentieth-century economy has produced the first culture for which a beggar is a reminder of nothing."[57] We feel Berger goes too far by exclusively blaming the rich for all poverty on earth today. The root causes of poverty are myriad, and include factors far beyond wealth distribution (e.g., public policy/governance, war, rule of law, and of course, responsible individual decision-making). Nevertheless, Berger rightly points out that our moral duty toward an injustice increases as our capacity to remedy that injustice increases.

None of this is to say that the reason we support the poor is because they are necessarily "deserving" of our generosity—who are we to decide that, anyway? Rather, we as Christians hold a moral duty to support the poor because the poor are fellow children of God, and because supporting our fellow brothers and sisters reflects God's nature, resulting in His glory.[58]

We let Saint Augustine present the closing argument: "Wherefore, as often as you are able to help others, and refuse, so often did you do them wrong."[59]

PRINCIPLE SIX: GIVING SHOULD BE VOLUNTARY, GENEROUS (EVEN SACRIFICIAL), CHEERFUL, AND NEEDS-BASED.

We explored the qualitative characteristics of giving taught in the New Testament in the previous chapter:

- Giving should be of free volition—we should not be coerced

---

57 As cited in Stearns, Richard. *The Hole in Our Gospel*, 95.

58 Moreover, as we discuss in later chapters, there are wise and effective ways to alleviate poverty.

59 As cited in Stearns, Richard. *The Hole in Our Gospel*, 268.

to give by authorities at our local church.[60]

- Giving should be done cheerfully as we recognize the spiritual blessings God pours out on those who give, since "God loves a cheerful giver."[61]

- Giving should be applied toward genuine community needs, specifically in support of local ministers and the poor.[62]

- Finally, giving should be generous, even sacrificial.[63]

The beauty of this mode of giving is that it frees Christians to generously serve others out of thankfulness to God for His provision. The challenge, however, is how exactly to define "generous."

The other characteristics of New Covenant giving are more straightforward: we know whether we have given voluntarily and cheerfully (though *becoming* a cheerful giver if we are not one can be more difficult). We also know whether our giving is supporting genuine community needs, such as providing for local pastors and the poor (if we do not know this, we as stewards ought to find out!). But knowing whether or not we have given generously is more ambiguous.

"How much should I give to be generous?" This question appears reasonable on the surface, but it in fact implies a works-based view of our relationship with God. "If I give *enough*, I will be doing *enough* to please God." Paul corrects this mistaken view in Ephesians 2:8-9: "For by grace you have been saved through faith. And this is not your own doing; it is the gift of God, not a result

---

60 2 Corinthians 8:3; 9:7

61 2 Corinthians 9:7; Malachi 3:10; Proverbs 3:9-10; Luke 6:38

62 1 Corinthians 9:3-14; 2 Corinthians 8:4-5; Acts 20:35; Matthew 25:31-45

63 2 Corinthians 8:2-3; Philippians 4:17-18; Mark 12:42-44

of works, so that no one may boast." It is not the amount we give that gains us favor in God's eyes—all "our" possessions are truly God's to begin with!

So, what does it mean to give generously? Recall our definition of stewardship: the active and responsible management of God's creation for God's purposes. What are God's purposes for us? We have always liked the Westminster Shorter Catechism's articulation of the chief end of Man: "to glorify God, and to enjoy Him forever."[64] Thus, our view is that giving generously is to give in such a way that God is glorified.

First Chronicles 29:9-14 provides a fantastic illustration of giving in such a way to glorify God. King David gives a massive offering to support the construction of God's temple; the king's gift inspires the people to make similar freewill offerings themselves: huge quantities of gold, silver, bronze, iron, and precious stones. The author captures King David's and the people's reaction:

> *"Then the people rejoiced because they had given willingly . . . David the king also rejoiced greatly.*
>
> *And David said: "Blessed are you, O Lord, the God of Israel our father, forever and ever. . . . Both riches and honor come from you, and you rule over all. . . . And now we thank you, our God, and praise your glorious name.*
>
> *But who am I, what is my people, that we should be able thus to offer willingly? For all things come from you, and of your own we have given you."*

Here we see that God is glorified when we give out of recognition of God's sovereignty over our wealth, out of gratitude for His provision, and out of joy in the opportunity to participate in His Kingdom. These are the foundational characteristics of generosity.

One might point out that King David and the Israelites also gave a very large *amount* in this example. However, generosity is not measured by the absolute amount we give. In the story of the Widow's Offering in Mark 12, Jesus commends a widow for giving all she had (two small copper coins) to the temple (Mark 12:41-44). Generosity is relative: in the eyes of Christ, the poor widow's two coins were "more" than the many rich peoples' "large sums." A. W. Tozer writes, "Before the judgment seat of Christ, my service will be judged not by how much I have done, but by how much I could have done."[65]

Giving generously is to give in such a way that God is glorified. God is glorified by our giving when we recognize His sovereignty, are grateful for His provision, and are joyful in our opportunity to serve Him. Finally, our giving must be commensurate with our means. Christ clearly honored the widow in Mark 12 who gave everything. What might "commensurate" look like for us today?

Principle Seven: Giving generously breaks the power of money over us.[66]

Shailer Matthews, an American theologian, quips that "if it is more blessed to give than to receive, then most of us are content to let the other fellow have the greater blessing."[67] Content as

---

65 Tozer, A. W. *That Incredible Christian*, 105.

66 We are grateful to Ron Blue for articulating this concept at a Kingdom Advisors conference we attended during our research.

67 Matthews, Shailer. As quoted by Generous Church at http://www.generouschurch.com/quotes-on-generosity. Accessed 3/19/15.

many of us may be to let the other fellow have the greater blessing, generosity is in fact critical to our own spiritual health. Benefits of generosity include increased joy, personal satisfaction from serving others, spiritual growth, and blessing from God, both now and in eternity.[68] Perhaps most importantly, giving generously breaks the power that money can so easily hold over us. We believe the idolatry of money is a serious temptation for many western Christians today, and it is on this topic that we focus our discussion.

Scripture warns us of the danger of worshipping Mammon.[69] Paul cautions us that "those who desire to be rich fall into temptation, into a snare, into many senseless and harmful desires that plunge people into ruin and destruction" (1 Timothy 6:9). King Solomon admonishes us that "He who loves money will not be satisfied with money, nor he who loves his wealth with his income" (Ecclesiastes 5:10). Jesus reminds us to "Take care, be on guard against all covetousness, for one's life does not consist in the abundance of his possessions" (Luke 12:15).

We so easily succumb to the notion that just a little more money will give us the life we always dreamed of. Ironically, this mistaken belief seems to intensify as we accumulate more wealth. A pastor once told us a story about a friend of his from college. Before they graduated, the two friends discussed how much money they wanted to earn in their careers in order to retire comfortably. They settled on an amount of five million dollars.[70] The pastor followed the career progression of his college friend, who was moving rapidly through the ranks of a well-known Fortune 500 company. Ten

---

68 Jones, Larry. "Five Benefits of Generosity." http://www.richchristianpoorchristian.com/2011/10/5-benefits-of-generosity.html. Accessed 3/21/15.

69 "Mammon" is a word used by Jesus in Matthew 6:24 and Luke 16:13. Thought to be based on the Aramaic word for riches or money, the word was used by early Christians to describe conspicuous consumption, excessive materialism, and greed. Jesus used the term as a personification of a false god in these passages.

70 This conversation took place before the pastor knew he would be called into vocational ministry!

years after graduation, the pastor called his friend and said, "I've been following your career. Do you remember our conversation? You must have hit five million dollars by now. How does it feel to be able to retire?" The friend replied, "You know, we were so naïve back then. The number isn't five million—it's 20 million! Life is more complicated than you realize."

The pastor continued to follow his friend's career. Twenty years after graduation, the friend was now CEO of a Fortune 500 company. The pastor called him again to ask the same question, and the CEO replied, "You know, I was so naïve back then. I'm above the number, but I can't retire yet! We just don't feel secure." This time, the CEO could not even articulate for what purpose the extra money would be used. In truth, the money was a drug, used to treat the CEO's insecurity about his self-worth and well-being. Ironically, the cause of the CEO's unbearable insecurity was the drug itself—his pursuit of wealth! Cyprian, bishop of Carthage in the third century, sums this up well: "Their property held them in chains. . . . They think of themselves as owners, whereas it is they rather who are owned: enslaved as they are to their own property, they are not the masters of their money but its slaves."[71]

Another consequence of the worship of money is that it often causes us to see the worst in others. We begin to look down upon the less fortunate—oftentimes even blaming them for their own misfortune. Authors Don McClanen and Dale Stitt argue that "[Money] becomes Mammon whenever our passion for nice things is stronger than our compassion for the wounded in our world."[72] Richard Stearns, President of World Vision, hammers home this point by paraphrasing The Final Judgment passage

---

71 Cyprian, quoted in Alcorn, Randy. Money, *Possessions, and Eternity*, 416.

72 McClanen and Stitt. *Ministry of Money*, 3.

in Matthew 25:31-45:

> *"For I was hungry, while you had all you needed. I was thirsty, but you drank bottled water. I was a stranger, and you wanted me deported. I needed clothes, but you needed more clothes. I was sick, and you pointed out the behaviors that led to my sickness. I was in prison, and you said I was getting what I deserved."*[73]

For a Closer Look . . .

To hear more from Richard Stearns about how we have fallen short of living according to biblical principles on finances, watch the 15-minute video, "Multiplex: Wealth, Poverty and Power - The Hole in our Gospel," at GodandMoney.net/resources.

This is not to say that responsible decision-making plays no role in one's financial well-being. Of course, it does! Even so, the love of wealth may foster an attitude of arrogance that causes us to lose our compassion for the poor; to fail to serve Jesus by failing to serve those whom He loves.

A final negative consequence of the worship of money is its ability to distort how we measure success in our lives. We begin to use money as a measuring stick for worldly success and self-worth. I (Greg) recall endless water cooler conversations about annual bonuses at both McKinsey and the private equity firm at which I worked. The bonus numbers at both firms were stratospheric by any objective standard, but my colleagues and I were not interested in discussing how fortunate we were to receive such large bonuses. Instead, we were interested in discussing how our bonus compared to our peers'. Rather than marveling at my good-fortune to receive

---

73 Stearns, Richard. *The Hole in Our Gospel*, 59.

a six-figure bonus as a twenty-something, I hurriedly asked my boss whether my bonus put me in the "top bucket" of employees or not. My bonus was nothing more than a signal of my value relative to my colleagues. I had unwittingly embraced the world's teaching that money makes us valuable. Dietrich Bonhoeffer counters this teaching: "In a world where success is the measure and justification of all things . . . the figure of the [Christ] Crucified invalidates all thought which takes success for its standard."[74] In other words, our value is found in Christ, not in our money.

The love of money causes us to become insecure, unsatisfied, and self-absorbed. It deceives us into embracing a false system for measuring our self-worth. Conversely, being generous with our wealth eliminates its power over us. Generously sharing our wealth with others protects us against falling into worship of Mammon and enables us to experience the unmatched joy of walking with Christ and participating in the redemption of God's Kingdom.

"EVERYTHING FLIPPED"—APPLYING THE BIBLICAL PRINCIPLES ON WEALTH AND GIVING

Distilling all God's teaching on wealth and money down to these seven principles enabled us to better understand His overall message. We began to coalesce around the insight that a faithful reading of Scripture leads not to the question "How much should I give?" but rather to the question "How much do I need to keep?" Flipping the question this way is a very countercultural thing to do, even within the church. But it is exactly the mindset we must embrace in order to truly honor God through our generosity.

---

74 Bonhoeffer, Dietrich. *Ethics*, 363.

Will Pope arrived at the same conclusion well before we did. Now in his mid-fifties, Will owns a successful oil and gas firm in Oklahoma City, Oklahoma. Will exudes a good-natured, "Aw, shucks" vibe that makes him instantly likable. Whenever we speak by phone, I imagine him leaning back in a big leather chair, propping his cowboy boots up on a big oaken desk, gazing at a big white steer skull on the wall. However, Will's friendly demeanor and affable sense of humor belie his seriousness with respect to a deeply rooted faith in Christ and his strong views on the nature of generosity.

Will's conviction on the topic of generosity is born out of the incredible journey on which God has carried him and his business. His journey begins in the year 1998, by which point Will had been running his business for 22 years. Will had been pouring himself into the company, and it was working: the company was growing and was turning a consistent profit. At the end of each year, Will would estimate his "balance sheet net worth" based on the prospective market value of his company. Each time he did this, the value crept higher and higher. All the blood, sweat, and tears Will had invested into the company were clearly paying off.

Eventually, though, his company's growth ceased to motivate Will. The bigger number he tabulated at the end of the year no longer excited him. He felt empty. Will eventually came to the conclusion that this emptiness was driven by his belief that his business had no eternal impact—that he was wasting his time, from a Kingdom perspective. "I wanted to make a difference," he says. In a bold attempt to store up more treasure in heaven, Will took a sabbatical from his business and moved his wife and two school-aged children to Costa Rica to explore the idea of becoming a missionary.

Will picks up the story:

> *We had been there only four weeks. I was still in [Spanish language] training. It was after school and we were having lunch at a small restaurant in San José. I was sitting with a fellow student who suddenly asked me, "Why are you here?"*
>
> *I answered out loud, "I'm thinking I should be a missionary." She looked at me funny. I get the sense she thought I was crazy.*
>
> *As soon as I had said this, I heard a voice speak clearly in my mind, "You think you learned all this on your own?" My brain rapid-fired. I immediately knew what the question meant. I was not formally educated as a businessman—I learned everything through experience. Or at least, that's what I thought. I actually started crying because I knew what the answer to God's question was. Then, as the tears came, my fellow student was convinced I was crazy!*
>
> *In that moment, I realized all that experience and learning had been God's providence over my life. I realized in that instant that my mission field is not being a missionary—it is using all the skills God has given me to go back into business. An incredible peace came over me. I realized God had put me in business for a reason. He had created a clear purpose for my life. God has given me great skills and resources, and I have to use them for Him. Before, I thought being a business person was unholy in some*

sense. After this event, I felt a clear calling on my life. Everything flipped. It flipped from "this is my deal" to "this is God's deal." I am free to make an eternally significant difference.

Leaving the training, Will returned home to run his business. Except now it was God's business. Will was no longer working for himself. Even though he was CEO, he now had a new Chairman. He became passionate about growing the company again because now any growth he achieved would directly support God's Kingdom. And the business started growing steadily. What was once a relatively small family-owned business was quickly becoming a sizable and rapidly growing enterprise.

Will's view on generosity was evolving alongside the growth of his company. He says,

I am at the Kindergarten level of this stuff. I really am not a naturally good giver. I am trying to get better at it. It is a constant struggle for me. I am not very generous, especially with concerns [about providing] for my family and worrying the business would blow up. We spent a lot of time developing different pots of money: college fund, retirement fund, "if-the-business-blows-up" account. Then, we had a windfall of $20,000 come our way all of a sudden. We felt called to give it away, but it was a huge gift for us to give. My wife, Rachel, always wanted to give it all away. I was the stingy one, wanting to continue to control it. I thought, "What if we set up a foundation, invest it, and give away the interest?" This is what we ended up doing. It was a little seed capital. Before long, though, we started *to give it all away, started putting more money into it. We started to get really serious about our giving.*

Will's giving strategy was supported by his newfound attitude toward his own wealth. He elaborates, "I don't think about the business as mine anymore. My focus changed from my net worth to a 'financial finish line' that is a real, quantifiable number." Will asked a few close Christian friends to become his financial advisors. Each year, his advisors set his "annual salary." Rather than taking all of the profits home himself, he now receives a set amount of compensation regardless of how well the company actually performs. All excess profits are given away. [75]

In recent years, Will's salary has been about $200,000 per year. Will confesses he is a bit embarrassed even by this number, though it is far below the actual profits generated by the company. At the same time, having his salary set for him has been very good for Will spiritually. He says,

> *The first feedback I got from my advisors is that I was too stingy with my family. For example, I remember telling my wife she could only buy store-brand food for our family. Ten cans of frozen orange juice for a dollar! I was mean to my wife, being really strict with the budget. She still suffers from [me treating her that way] to this day. I learned that generosity means you need to be generous with your family as well. Of course, it's a balance—you can be "too generous" with your family as well. The key is to have good financial coaches who love us.*

---

75 Here, we actually mean cash flow after accounting for capital expenditures invested back in the business.

To serve God in a variety of ways, Will utilizes the excess profits from his company including several creative forms of generosity that extend beyond traditional giving. For example, he pays his employees well above market rates and hires interns every summer in order to give them valuable experience. He also regularly places anonymous envelopes on cars in public parking lots all over town. The envelopes include $20 and a card which reads "Love is all it takes. Live your life in love. You are a recipient of an intentional act of grace, love, and kindness. Will you pay it forward?" Will's goal is to leave one such envelope on a car every day.

Working with his advisors, Will determined a "finish line" with respect to his retirement savings. Once his savings hit his finish line number, he stopped saving. He believes he doesn't need any more, and there is no reason to save any additional money. He skims any capital gains on his "finish line" fund into his and his wife's foundation to be given away.

Will acknowledges that the process of selecting a finish line is a little "fuzzy." He selected his finish line based on his and his wife's age, the needs of his grandchildren, expected future financial obligations, etc. In fact, Will's advisors thought the initial finish line he proposed was too conservative—they recommended he increase it by 20 percent. Will elaborates, "I am so concerned about not being a good steward. There is no right method at the end of the day. You need good counsel. There are so many variables. At different times in your life, things will change. You need to continually revisit it. Be prepared to be flexible. You can find the right answer for your family. If your heart is in the right place, you can't make a bad decision."

By the way, the value of Will's business is not included in his finish line. He isn't thinking about selling the business anytime soon, but if he does, the proceeds will be given to God. He says, "I haven't done a net worth/balance sheet since setting up our finish line. The business isn't mine anymore."

Each of the Seven Core Principles of Biblical Wealth and Giving presented in this chapter are evident in Will's story. Will's story is inspiring because he has actually made it God's story. By "flipping" his understanding of God's provision, Will recognized that everything he has—even the company itself—rightly belongs to God. He has lived out this realization in all areas of his life, from his salary, to his savings, to his giving, to how he runs his business.

Will realized that asking "How much should I give?" not only sold God short, but also sold *himself* short by detracting from his ability to enjoy the blessings God pours out on those who are generous (Luke 6:38). He implemented his own version of "How much do I need to keep?" and hasn't looked back since. Will finally feels free to play his role in God's Kingdom. His business is not actually his anymore, and that's alright with him. After all, "It's not about me," Will concludes. "It's all about God."

CHAPTER THREE

Motivations for Giving

*"Our worship of God is deeper precisely because of,
not in spite of, our philosophical studies."*

—J. P. Moreland and William Lane Craig

The first four Core Principles for Biblical Wealth and Giving are normative, spiritual truths of the Christian faith. You either accept these on the authority of the Bible, or you don't. It would be pointless, for example, to debate on the evidence whether heavenly wealth is eternal or not. If you believe in Jesus as Savior, you'll accept this teaching from the Bible; and if you don't, then you won't. The last three principles, however, make claims and suggest behaviors that can be tested and empirically verified. We thought it would be worth asking whether they hold water when viewed through a sociological, philosophical, or medical lens. Whenever it's possible, a truth claim should be exposed to the evidence to see whether it can stand the test of hard scrutiny. We wanted to do this for the principles we had discovered in Scripture. If they are true, there is no reason to shy away from scrutiny, and if they are false, well, perhaps we would need to revisit our interpretations.

Applying scientific scrutiny to religious claims makes many people antsy. Christianity, however, is unique in that its core precepts hinge on historical realities that can in fact be investigated. Indeed, Paul writes that "if Christ has not been raised . . . your faith is in vain" (1 Corinthians 15:14). Thankfully, there is compelling evidence for the literal and historical resurrection of Jesus,[76] but our purpose is not to discuss that here. We're focused on money.

As a side note, we believe this is where the prosperity gospel comes up short. If giving money makes God rain down material blessings on you, then why are there many faithful lower-income givers who continue to be lower-income year after year? Some might say that their faith is not big enough. We would say, however, that expecting riches as a reward for generosity is simply wrong based on both the Scriptures and realities we can observe in life today. According to the Seven Core Principles, a lower-income, generous family is being obedient to Scripture, fulfilling their moral obligation to this broken and hurting world, and will receive spiritual blessings for their generosity. However, expecting a material or financial windfall would be unrealistic.

The first part of this chapter will focus on testing Principle Five, the moral obligation to give to the poor. By analyzing other faith traditions and the writings of a few prominent philosophers, we can contextualize our Christian paradigm and sharpen our vocabulary around the position we hold. Doing so increases our ability to have conversations with non-Christians—after all, who disagrees with generosity?

Afterward, we'll take a look at Principle Six, which relates to the way we should give (voluntarily, cheerfully, generously, and needs-based), and Principle Seven, which says that doing so will

---

76 An excellent primer to this topic and many others in apologetics can be found in William Lane Craig's book, *Reasonable Faith*. Chapter 8 deals with the resurrection.

free us from the power of money over us, enhancing our well-being. While empirical evidence regarding the spiritual benefits of giving is hard to come by, there is well-documented research on the physical and mental health of generous givers, and it is to this body of evidence we will turn.

After examining these three giving principles, we'll move ahead and review current trends in generosity. We suspect that the Holy Spirit is up to something very interesting in our particular moment of history, awakening a broad swathe of people, both young and old, to the unexpected joy of giving. We hope to be used by the Lord to spread this message further, unlocking new levels of generosity for the glory of Christ's name.

THE MORAL CASE FOR GENEROSITY: TESTING PRINCIPLE FIVE

As Christians, we often inhabit a philosophical bubble in which outside traditions remain unexamined. This is a bit tragic for two reasons. First, when we are unaware of what nonbelievers think and believe, our ability to engage with culture from an apologetic standpoint is seriously undermined. Secondly, as C. S. Lewis points out in *Mere Christianity*, Christians are free to engage with and affirm truth within all human traditions. When non-Christians derive truth, the Christian should celebrate, because the ultimate realities of God that are written on every human heart are simply finding their expression. (Take, for example, the notion of servant leadership. While a distinctively Christian notion, we rejoice when we see it applied in society.) It is, therefore, worth asking what other belief systems and philosophical frameworks have to say about generosity.

RELIGIONS

It is a rare day when Eastern faiths, Abrahamic faiths, and atheism all agree wholeheartedly on something. Take your pick of worldview, however, and we'll bet that it encourages sharing from your abundance with others. While we cannot accurately capture a belief system in a single quote, we have selected relevant statements on giving from the major non-Christian belief systems.

Atheism: "Let us try to teach generosity and altruism, because we are born selfish." —Richard Dawkins

Buddhism: "Teach this triple truth to all: A generous heart, kind speech, and a life of service and compassion are the things which renew humanity." —Siddhartha Gautama (Buddha)

Confucianism: "He who wishes to secure the good of others has already secured his own." —Confucius

Hinduism: "They who give, have all things; they who withhold have nothing." —Hindu Proverb

Islam: "You shall never be truly righteous until you give in alms what you dearly cherish." —Qur'an Al-Imran

Judaism: "Whoever loves money never has enough; whoever loves wealth is never satisfied with his income. This too is meaningless." —King Solomon, Book of Ecclesiastes

Virtually all of humanity, it turns out, values generosity. There is something fundamentally and unavoidably human about the need to share our resources for the good of others! If God takes this issue very seriously, then it makes sense that it would attract unanimous agreement throughout humanity.

Secular Moral Philosophy

We now turn to a closer look at the moral philosophy of giving from a secular perspective, in order to glean and appreciate aspects of truth where we may find them, and improve our ability to engage with secular culture on the topic.

While the major world religions influence the masses, most of the intellectual elites of the world today are more influenced by secular philosophers. We'll spend a few pages with some giants of philosophy, whose teachings undergird much of what is taught at universities today in the realm of ethics and morality. If Christians want to influence culture at a macro level, we must understand how our culture's leading thinkers view the subject of generosity. (At one point we found ourselves discussing radical generosity with an atheist in the Harvard library, and discovered that being able to switch back and forth between utilitarian philosophy and Christian Scriptures can be very handy!)

The Modern Philosopher of Ethics:
Peter Singer

We turn first to Peter Singer, an atheist at Princeton University and one of the most prominent ethical philosophers of the modern day, who espouses preference utilitarianism. This ethical framework holds that there are no universal moral principles, and that morality is founded on maximizing the subjective preferences of all sentient beings. On the basis of this system, he advocates for many positions which Christians find reprehensible—indeed, there is much for a Christian and an atheist to argue over—but we share common ground with him on the issue of financial generosity.

On the specific issue of giving, Singer penned an article in 1971 entitled "Famine, Affluence, and Morality"[77] which became quite famous and was later expanded into a book entitled *The Life You Can Save*.[78] Singer questions the notion of "charity" to begin with, as if giving from the rich of the world to the poor of the world is even praiseworthy. Giving is not a positive act of goodness, he claims, but rather the fulfilment of a basic human duty. Singer basically claims that giving is like bathing. Nobody gets a gold medal for doing it, yet we see it as a personal failure if someone doesn't do it! Through this lens, inaction, or a lack of giving, becomes a moral failure.

Singer famously presents an analogy to demonstrate this view: when you walk past a child drowning in a shallow pond, there is an ethical obligation for you to intervene. When the need is great (a child is drowning) and the cost of relieving the need is minimal (your clothes get muddy), it is a moral imperative to act. The only difference between this analogy and present-day charitable giving is that:

1. The needy are far away

2. There are millions of them

3. Many other people also have the ability to save them

Singer argues that the distance between you and the needy is irrelevant. Discrimination on the basis of distance, when helping out is as easy as an online donation, makes no moral sense.

The number of needy is also a poor excuse for inaction. The fact that 100 children are drowning in the pond is no excuse for a man to continue walking past on the grounds that he cannot save them all. It is his duty to save as many as he can.

---

77 Singer, Peter, "Famine, Affluence, and Morality." http://www.utilitarian.net/singer/by/1972—.htm, accessed October 2014.

78 Singer, Peter, *The Life You Can Save*. (Random House); http://www.thelifeyoucansave.org/, accessed October 2014.

Finally, the fact that other people could be helping might make us feel less guilty for standing idly by, but it does not reduce our moral duty. If many onlookers surround the pond but do nothing, is it right to simply join in and watch the child drown?

Singer acknowledges that his arguments, taken to their logical conclusion, suggest charitable giving of a magnitude far beyond what is customary in the modern Western world. He draws upon Thomas Aquinas for support,[79] (an atheist quoting a Catholic—don't you love how we all agree on this topic?) emphasizing that thinkers throughout history have endorsed the notion that the excess wealth of the rich, when hoarded for personal benefit, is effectively stolen from the poor. This stands in stark contrast to our modern emphasis on increasing personal consumption. It is noteworthy how closely the views of Singer, an atheistic philosopher, correspond with the views on wealth found in the Bible. We disagree on issues like abortion and sexual ethics, but find common ground when it comes to wealth and giving. Lives lived in self-oriented luxury are condemned, and we must lament the fact that the poor continue living in a desperate state without relief.

> ## For a Closer Look . . .
>
> Peter Singer gave a TED talk on effective altruism which has over one million views. As Christians we may disagree violently with him on some issues, but we can agree with his heart for generosity toward the least of these. Check out his 17-minute talk, "The Why and How of Effective Altruism," at GodandMoney.net/resources.

In his own words, Singer explains the problem with our society's view of giving: "The charitable man may be praised, but the man who is not charitable is not condemned. People do not feel in any

---

79 Singer, "Famine, Affluence, and Morality."

way ashamed or guilty about spending money on new clothes or a new car instead of giving it to famine relief. (Indeed, the alternative does not occur to them.) This way of looking at the matter cannot be justified."[80] This sounds strikingly similar to Jesus, speaking to the wealthy church of Laodicea through the apostle John in Revelation 3:17, "For you say, I am rich, I have prospered, and I need nothing, not realizing that you are wretched, pitiable, poor, blind, and naked." There are key differences between Christian giving and utilitarian giving,[81] but the two perspectives share in their lambasting of those who are wealthy and closed off to the cry of the poor.

Singer gives 20 to 25 percent of his income away, but suggests that it would be morally right to give even more. He states that if all of the world's affluent gave just one percent of their income to fight extreme poverty, it would be more than double what governments currently contribute and could eradicate extreme poverty from the earth.[82]

Before we move on, we just want to point out how much this stung us. Earning six figures before business school, we each chose to give 10 to 15 percent away. We are Christians, called to love the world by the God that we worship. Meanwhile, an atheist professor at Princeton was giving more than 20 percent? Motivated by nothing but a utilitarian concern for his fellow man? With no belief in the afterlife or in a God that was telling him to do it? Ouch.

---

80 Ibid.

81 Notably, Christian giving is out of response to God's freely given grace, and is full of joy and purpose because of this. Utilitarian giving, while perhaps leading to a "helper's high," cannot rest upon a desire for eternal joy, given an atheistic denial of an afterlife. Also, Christian teaching on money allows for the steward of wealth to enjoy the fruit of his labor, whereas utilitarian giving demands giving down to the point of marginal utility—or giving unto the point of poverty, essentially, to be perfectly ethical. Finally, atheist utilitarian giving focuses on alleviating material poverties. Christian giving agrees with this, but also includes the alleviation of spiritual poverty through the spreading of the Gospel.

82 Singer, Peter. "Extending Generosity to the Wider World," http://www.utilitarianism.net/singer/by/20020630.htm, accessed October 2014.

The Enlightenment Philosopher of Ethics: Immanuel Kant

Before ending our foray into philosophy (we'll be done soon, we promise) we turn to Immanuel Kant, a giant of the enlightenment. Kant's personal views on generosity reflect some degree of nuance. He was generally opposed to alms-giving, or the passing of funds to beggars, because the whole situation felt messy to him.[83] The beggar loses his dignity and agency by begging and is demeaned in the process. Further, the one giving to the beggar usually just gives because they feel awkward and guilty. Pure and proper motivation to act ethically, which was very important to Kant, is missing from the whole situation.

Many generous acts, however, are indeed ethical in Kant's worldview. His overall views on wealth transfers from the rich to the poor are similar to Aquinas' and Singer's—that the wealthy are merely returning a portion of what belonged to the poor in the first place. His logic is as follows: [84]

1. The rich are only rich insofar as they have property rights.

2. Property rights are guaranteed by a state, whose function is to provide order and justice to society.

3. Proper administration of justice by the state includes the obligation to ensure no one is in abject poverty.

4. Abject poverty is thus a failure of the state.

5. The rich, then, obtained their wealth under the protection of a partially failed state, which helped them get rich while failing to prevent abject poverty.

---

83 Allais, Lucy, "Kant on Giving to Beggars," University of the Witwatersrand, http://wiser.wits.ac.za/system/files/seminar/Allais2012.pdf, accessed October 2014.

84 Ibid.

6. Therefore, a portion of the wealth of the rich should have gone to the poor in the first place, if the state was appropriately administering order and justice.

Thus, riches are to some extent a result of injustice to the poor; a misappropriation of property by an imperfectly functioning government. At this point in our journey, the whole "let's study philosophy" thing was really beginning to hurt. These non-Christian philosophers had some good points, and they were beating up on us. Is Kant really saying that the money we gave to our churches and to global poverty actually belonged to the poor in the first place, in an indirect sense? We had felt pretty good about our tithing, but it was beginning to sound like we were morally obligated to give that money to begin with. Maybe secular philosophy is stricter than most sermons preached on Stewardship Sunday . . . If we thought our pastors were tough on money, we should have checked out a philosophy book from the local library!

In the Kantian framework giving to the poor is the right thing to do but it is not necessarily praiseworthy. We were hoping that such a view might have died with Kant, which would be awfully convenient given our own plans for spending our future salaries. Unfortunately for us, this view was adopted and espoused by none other than the steel magnate Andrew Carnegie, who accumulated one of the largest fortunes in history and subsequently gave it all away. In *The Gospel of Wealth* he writes, "the millionaire will be but a trustee for the poor; entrusted for a season with a great part of the increased wealth of the community."[85] He believed that after meeting their own material needs, the wealthy come into a moral obligation to return their fortunes to society in the most efficient manner possible.

---

85 Andrew Carnegie, "The Gospel of Wealth," North American Review, http://www.swarthmore.edu/SocSci/rbannis1/AIH19th/Carnegie.html, June, 1889. Accessed November 2014.

PHILOSOPHY CONCLUSIONS

In the ethics of generosity, then, there is a tension between competing frameworks. Peter Singer's utilitarianism argues for optimizing flourishing in an algorithmic fashion, but in some cases such as Kant's analysis of beggars, this seems to encroach upon individual agency and ignore moral complexity. Interestingly, this same tension is present in the Christian Scriptures. Christian teaching suggests that wealth is a powerful temptation to idolatry, that God is the ultimate owner of all wealth, and that wealth frequently springs from injustice. However, wealth is also praised as a reward for labor.[86] We do not find in Scripture a condemnation of the rich simply for being rich—condemnation is reserved for those who are blind to the plight of the less fortunate, and those who become proud. There is a dynamic tension between the constantly repeated call to help the poor and the understanding that wealth exists to serve the human needs and enjoyment of those who have worked hard for it.

As we studied and researched, we began to feel that perhaps this tension contains a profound wisdom; a dynamic ethical convergence between the traditions of Christian faith and secular Western moral philosophy. Each tradition might disagree profoundly on the decision frameworks one should use in evaluating a giving plan, the ultimate amount one should give, and the particular motivations that should animate the giver. They converge, however, in Aristotelean moderation on the issue of wealth. We shouldn't let guilt drive us to relinquish all material possessions, nor should we let greed inspire us to consume all that we can earn. When looking at our own hearts and the trends in American society, however, we realized that our giving is probably far short of what a fair reading of almost any tradition would recommend. As believers, we

---

86 These points are summarized from a lecture by Harvey Cox at Harvard Divinity School, September, 2014.

concluded that we can encourage all wealthy Westerners, not just Christians, to give more than they do now on the basis of widely held philosophical beliefs. Whether someone likes utilitarian atheism, the enlightenment, Christianity, or something else . . . they can find a compelling reason to give generously.

Looking ahead to our golden-handcuff salaries, we realized that if we installed a smaller swimming pool, shaved 300 square feet off our custom floor plans, spent one less day on our nice vacations, or drove a Toyota instead of a Lexus, we could save lives and spread the Gospel. There is not much moral tension in these decisions, but we simply choose to ignore the question. We choose to consume and to create a culture of consumerism, over and over and over again, until we find ourselves trapped on a treadmill of spending and wealth accumulation. We both realized that this was the direction we were headed with our lives. Our case studies, which spoke powerfully into our hearts, stand in stark contrast to the prevailing culture of over-indulgence and excess, perhaps speaking a much-needed word to our society: that we need to reach beyond ourselves and do something of eternal significance with our vast Western wealth.

We are grateful that you, our reader, have allowed us to take you on our journey of philosophical exploration. We hope it was profitable for you—it was convicting for us. We also hope it helps bolster your confidence in Principle Five, derived from Scripture and, as we have seen, supported by centuries of human philosophy from many angles. Generosity is indeed our moral obligation to a hurting world, and even those who profess no God feel the pull of their conscience in this area of human affairs. When engaging with Christians, we can speak the language of the Bible. When speaking with secular society, however, we can engage with other tools of argumentation that contain kernels of the same truths.

THE MEDICAL CASE FOR GENEROSITY: TESTING PRINCIPLES 6 AND 7

Oh, my dear Christians! If you would be like Christ, give much, give often, give freely, to the vile and the poor, the thankless and the undeserving. Christ is glorious and happy, and so will you be. It is not your money I want, but your happiness. Remember his own word: "It is more blessed to give than to receive."
—Sermon by R. M. McCheyne, 1838

There are two reasons why people do things that they don't like doing. First, some unpleasant tasks are in our own self-interest. Most of us don't get a dopamine rush out of brushing our teeth every morning, yet we all do it. Why? Well, we like our teeth, and the long-term planner in each of us knows that if we fail to engage in this daily discipline, we won't have them in 20 years.

The second reason to do something you don't enjoy is that it helps society get along. This is why we pick up our own trash in a public park. Again, most of us aren't getting a big rush out of stooping over to grab that loose piece of plastic that flies off the picnic table, yet we all do it. Why? Well, we all understand at some basic level that society needs us to. We all know that if nobody cleaned up their trash, the park would be unusable. So we all do our part.

Giving, for most people, feels like it belongs in the second category of activities— something you do out of obligation, to help society get along. You might even get this impression after reading the philosophy section. If our money partially belongs to the poor anyway, and we have a duty to give, perhaps we should just suck it up and do our part. Unfortunately, there is no joy in this mindset, and it is thus ineffective at changing behavior. Six out of seven

American families give less than two percent of their income.[87] For these families, giving is sort of like throwing up a karmic Hail-Mary every now and then—buying a cake from the bake sale "for the kids," or writing a $50 check out of peer pressure to support a college student's summer volunteer project, etc. Maybe if these families feel especially guilty one Sunday, they drop $20 in the offering plate. But giving is likely not a structured part of their lives.

What if, however, evidence began to emerge that giving was in the first category? What if stinginess could kill you just as quickly and silently as smoking a pack a day, and generosity was just as healthy and gave you a big rush of energy like going out for a daily jog? As you might have guessed, that's exactly where we are heading in this section, and the evidence turns out to be powerful and compelling. After the moral beating we had received from the philosophers, we were eager for some good news on the giving front.

For a comprehensive treatment of this topic we recommend the work of the Science of Generosity project, based out of the University of Notre Dame. In particular, *The Paradox of Generosity* by Christian Smith and Hilary Davidson is a resource we would recommend to anyone interested in exploring this topic in detail. What findings have emerged thus far?

First of all, giving is good for you. Really good for you. Intentional and regular practices of generosity have been associated with the release of a slew of good chemicals, including oxytocin, dopamine, and various endorphins. These chemicals are the same ones released after a hard workout or after a particularly pleasurable experience. In fact, generosity is strongly and clearly associated with a sense of purpose in life, personal happiness, and overall personal health. Giving, it turns out, lifts up human health as much as aspirin protects the heart. Finally, giving even activates the same portion

---

87 Christian Smith and Michael O. Emerson, "Passing the Plate," Oxford University Press, 2008.

of the brain that lights up when winning the lottery or getting a raise. You may not be able to control when you get a raise, but you can feel just as good simply by engaging in regular, consistent generosity. If Singer, Kant, Aquinas, and Carnegie are going to make us do it, we might as well be able to enjoy it!

Conversely, a lack of giving is bad for you. Those who do not regularly give have been found to harbor higher levels of the stress hormone cortisol, which has a linkage to everything from headaches, to stroke, to depression. What other areas suffer when we live ungenerously? How about pain management, body temperature regulation, blood pressure, and the control of fear?[88,][89] Living self-indulged and self-absorbed lives is literally killing us in the affluent West. As the authors put it:

> *Americans who do not give away 10 percent of their income run the significant risk of ending up less happy than they might have otherwise been. In fact, as a group they are less happy. So, whatever Americans lose by giving away 10 percent of their income is offset by the greater likelihood of being happier in life. . . . Rather than leaving generous people on the short end of an unequal bargain, practices of generosity are actually likely instead to provide generous givers with essential goods in life—happiness, health, and purpose—which money and time simply cannot buy. That is an empirical fact well worth knowing.[90]*

For many, the preceding paragraphs might be an inspiration to go write a $1,000 check in order to quickly grab the health benefits

---

88   R. Bodnar and G. Klein, "Endogenous Opiates and Behavior: 2003," Peptides 25, no. 12 (2004): 2205–2256.

89   Marques and Sternberg, "The Biology of Positive Emotions and Health," 164.

90   Christian Smith and Hilary Davidson, "The Paradox of Generosity," Oxford University Press, 2014.

of giving, without having to change their way of thinking or living. Unfortunately, this would not work, for the same reason that eating one healthy meal will not help us shed pounds gained from ongoing poor dietary habits. The type of generosity that is correlated with good outcomes is the kind that springs from a mindset of abundance and gratitude over the long-term, not the kind that comes from a sense of guilt or obligation. So what we need is a Gospel-centered revolution in our way of thinking! For us, this was welcome news. Having the philosophers squeeze money out of our paycheck with a moral guilt trip didn't sound very enjoyable. If we could discover how to find this generous mindset, maybe that would be a better way to go.

To give some examples of what works and what doesn't, simply being nice to people and smiling at strangers is not enough. Giving away 100 percent of your possessions in your will is not enough—allocating money to charity in a will is useless as far as positive outcomes go. Giving blood when your company asks you to is not enough, nor is faking a generous heart. Generosity that soothes the soul and heals the body is generosity that is integrated into one's lifestyle, material to the giver, and joyfully done out of an attitude of abundance. These are the conclusions reached by the Science of Generosity initiative after studying more than 2,000 Americans.

Is this sounding familiar? Principle Six, derived from Scripture, states that giving should be voluntary, generous (even sacrificial), cheerful, and needs-based. And Principle Seven claims that giving generously is critical for our spiritual health, freeing us from bondage to money. It seems that modern science has, in this case, verified what Scripture has been claiming for thousands of years.

As we wrapped up our deep dive into verifying Principles Five, Six, and Seven empirically, wondering how we could learn to give joyfully, we found ourselves in the middle of some very relevant conversations with Denise Whitfield, a financial advisor in Seattle. Talking with Denise is a joyful experience. She crafts phrases with careful and fluid gracefulness, helping conversations to flow along effortlessly. Within minutes, you feel like she is a friend you've known for ages. But there is more behind Denise's jubilance than good conversational skills. The currents of joy rushing underneath the surface of her heart are all but visible as you get to know her. She is the eldest of our newfound friends, at 61, yet manages to exude perhaps the greatest sense of adventure in life out of anyone we met during our journey. Her sense of joy springs from a "mindset of abundance," as she puts it—something that God spent many years teaching her. Naturally, we were curious to learn more.

Denise was raised by a Christian father and a religiously uncommitted mother. She never really considered herself a Christian until the age of 16, when she encountered some "Jesus People" in a coffee house, and through them, met Jesus as her personal savior. As she entered adulthood, marrying at 21, the world seemed to be nothing but an exciting upward climb into increasingly rarified social and economic company. She and her husband did well professionally and came to enjoy living the lifestyle of the Joneses, so to speak. Attending Harvard Business School was a memorable experience that cemented Denise's place in what she saw as an exciting, elite world. As she put it, "I felt as though I had been handed the golden keys to the kingdom, and was now among the 'accepted ones.' It was beguiling."

During the ensuing decades, as Denise and her husband raised their children, they were tithers or at least almost-tithers. It always seemed to be a struggle to hit the 10 percent number, but they nevertheless gave faithfully. To us, this sounded familiar based on our pre-business school giving patterns. At the high-income, high-society church they were attending, it was perhaps more common to hear people comparing their most recent exotic vacation than discussing the Gospel. As she approached 50 in the midst of this community, Denise felt God begin to call her to seek a deeper spiritual walk than she had before. She began to journal, to embrace times of meditation and solitude, and to wait before God in expectation, seeking whatever He had in store for her. During a period of several years, the Holy Spirit revealed that fear had been the dominant force in her life. Fear of not having enough, fear of not fitting in, fear of a million different things that could go wrong. She realized that her whole life had been driven by what she called a "scarcity mindset"—the need to protect and preserve; to cling to her possessions and opportunities lest they slip away in a moment of inattention.

Thankfully, as she surrendered her heart to God and continued seeking His presence through her spiritual disciplines, the abundance mindset began to replace the fear-driven scarcity mindset. She reflects that during this period, she felt the Lord call her to "Go deeper . . . and deeper still. You are safe with me, no matter what else happens. You can always go deeper into My presence."

It was truly God's sovereignty that prepared Denise in this way, because soon after this transformation her husband lost his high-paying corporate job. Suddenly, the Whitfield family was unable to live the high-flying lifestyles of their friends. As a matter of necessity, they cut consumption dramatically, tightening the belt to get through a period of relative hardship. Surprisingly, the friends they thought they knew so well seemed to all vanish from their lives. If a brother or sister in Christ fails to remain close to you when you can't fly away to a winter vacation home, how strong was the friendship to begin with? It became clear rather quickly which people Denise and her husband could retain strong relationships with, and those people tended to be those who spent a mere fraction of what their former circle did.

Despite the fact that the Whitfields were successfully adjusting to their newly reduced budget, some of their wealthier friends bungled an attempt at reaching out to them, awkwardly offering to bring by food for them to eat in case they couldn't afford groceries at Christmas-time. Denise did not need free groceries—she needed friends to stand with her in solidarity in a time of lifestyle adjustment. While they meant no harm, the insensitivity of her friends ("You can't afford European vacations any more? Poor thing, here's some grocery money.") caused Denise to vow never to become detached through a high-spending lifestyle again.

Denise moved on from this experience, remarkably free from any bitterness toward those who abandoned her when she could no longer live according to their standards of an acceptable lifestyle. She and her husband found new friends and a new way to live. With a mindset of abundance firmly in place, she actually found that her joy was stronger in this time of financial difficulty than it had been before, as she shifted her trust and put it all in God rather than material things.

With an empty nest at home and reduced income for her family, Denise decided to return to work. She eventually found a home in the financial advising business and has experienced rapid ascension and remarkable success. After the hard lessons learned about the false allure of conspicuous consumption, her spending has remained at a low level relative to the past. She and her husband decided that they would draw a line at which they were happy—not too far over $100,000 per year—and pretend that was all they earned. If they earned many multiples of that number, the upside would all be given away to the Lord's work. Because of her abundance mindset, Denise is not worried about saving more aggressively for retirement or legacy concerns. Any saving she does is done from within her lifestyle limit, which she regards as "enough," and the excess is entirely given away. Denise has earned much more than her lifestyle limit in recent years, yet she sticks to her plan with a spirit of joy and adventure. Her ambitions around giving have grown as her giving budget has gotten large. She reflects that the heart transformation she had in her forties was the key ingredient to her happy state today. Without such an internal change, she would have begun spending her higher income each year, and would today be in the same place she was in so many years before. Giving, for Denise, is a natural outflow of her internal mentality, rather than a response to a bunch of philosophical or moral imperatives. She gives not because a book told her to, but because she experienced a freedom through Christ which made it impossible to live any other way.

She reflects on the crowd that she left behind: "I've accepted that I may not meet the expectations of those who live a very wealthy lifestyle. Different interests, different worlds. They were so concerned with their pursuits that there was very little time to dig in for meaningful conversations, to get under the surface. It would be nice to occasionally talk about something other than the latest vacation, the newest house, or the problem with the decorator." It is amazing to see how she views a way of living that used to consume her with bemusement and an outsider's curiosity, despite now earning quite enough to rejoin that crowd if she chose to. Rather than looking socially upwards to try and stretch her lifestyle, Denise now looks outwards to the world, giving generously of herself to assist those in need. We believe that Denise's journey is a wonderful illustration of how the Gospel can bring to life the joy of generosity in someone's heart.

Research on giving, as you saw earlier in this chapter, points to the many benefits of generosity, including health effects. We asked Denise if she felt that the heart change she had experienced had impacted areas of life other than just finances. She immediately lit up and exclaimed, "I'm a completely different physical person! The scarcity mindset was linked to a lifelong battle with food. When God set me free from fear, I began losing weight." Today, she is 50 pounds lighter than she was before she began her journey of abundance with the Lord. While we would never promote financial giving as a weight-loss strategy, in Denise's case there were powerful links between her scarcity mindset and her dietary habits. When God set her free, everything changed! While this may look different for each person, we believe it is true that a mindset of abundance reaches deep into the human psyche, bringing new life on multiple levels.

As she told her story, we assumed that Denise had read *The Paradox of Generosity*, because the two words of contrast she chose, "scarcity" and "abundance," are key to the message and vocabulary of that book.

In the book, the authors address how a person's mindset dictates their perceived status. For example, someone with a mindset of abundance likely views the world as a place of blessing, sufficiency, and overflow, whereas a scarcity mindset probably causes them to see the world as a place of deficiency, vulnerability, and insecurity. Such perceptions are poorly correlated with someone's actual wealth or level of provision, but rather relate to underlying mental processes.[91]

Interestingly, Denise had not read the book. Those words are simply the best way to describe the prevailing mindset in society today, versus the mindset of freedom and hope found among those

---

91 Smith and Davidson, *"The Paradox of Generosity,"* 74.

surrendered to the truths of Christ. We had read the book on the benefits of an abundance mindset; she had lived it. After our conversations, Denise reflected deeply on her own conversation from a scarcity mindset to an abundance mindset and how it set her free spiritually. She sent us this poem that she wrote after one of our phone conversations on the scarcity mindset that "pulls us away from generosity."

> *Scarcity*
> *Painful*
> *It grabs at him*
> *Robs joy*
> *Lies to him*
> *It roars and complains*
> *Whines and whimpers*
> *Is never satisfied*
> *Pouts*
> *Denies God*
> *Embraces conspiracy*
> *Finally wins*
> *And he is lost*

I (John) recognized myself in Denise's tragic words about the scarcity mindset. In my desire for security and a blissful future state of early retirement, I had lost sight of the wonderful value and freedom available through Christ today. My world was all about the future and all about what I could build. My MBA was a surefire way to secure a six-figure income forever—a fail-safe safety net. Philosophies and Scriptures that denounced a self-absorbed lifestyle seemed like an inconvenience that I had to overcome, rather than a call to a heart-change. Denise's testimony continues to work on my heart as I seek after God's will for my finances and my life more generally—seeking the internal transformation that she had and that has been studied by the Science of Generosity initiative. My hope, before this project began, was to grab as much as I could for myself and my family and sock it away, but this false hope has slowly given way to a grander vision of sharing in God's Kingdom-building work in the world. Every now and then I look back at her poem, think about her story, and remind myself to be thankful that my Lord has abundantly met my every need.

CHAPTER FOUR

Trends and Movements in Generosity

"There are three conversions a person must experience: the conversion of the head, the conversion of the heart, and the conversion of the pocketbook."

—Martin Luther, paraphrase

So far, we have reviewed the Scriptures, distilled Core Principles from them, and also learned how giving is a good decision from both a moral and a medical perspective. Despite these motivations, however, the statistics show that American Christians simply do not give away very much money. If these principles accurately represent what the Bible teaches about wealth and money, we should expect

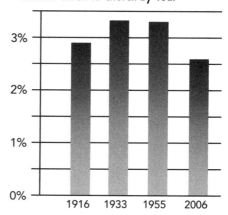

Table 2: Percent of American Protestants' Income Given to Church by Year

Christians to be giving generously, to be supporting the poor, and to be honoring God with our wealth. Yet unfortunately, Table 2 and Table 3 describe consistently low giving patterns in America over the last century.[92]

Table 3: Charitable Giving as Percent of Income by Income Bracket

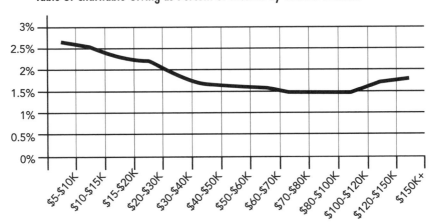

Additional surveys conducted by Christian Smith and Hilary Davidson at the University of Notre Dame indicate that less than three percent of American adults give away ten percent or more of their income, which many would consider a minimal baseline of true generosity.[93] These data paint a sober picture. Giving in America has remained flat as a percentage of income for the last century, despite the massive increase in average quality of life enjoyed by most Americans during this time period.

Under almost any definition, it is difficult to describe these patterns as "generous" when considering the quality of life enjoyed by most Americans today, especially those blessed to sit on the right-hand side of Table 3. Smith and Davidson summed it up well in the first line of their study: "America has a generosity problem."

---

92 For these statistics, see Empty Tomb, Inc., "The State of Giving Through 2006."

93 Smith and Davidson. "Giving Makes Us Happy. So Why Do So Few Do It?" http://generosityresearch. nd.edu/news/53522-giving-makes-us-happy-then-why-do-so-few-do-it/. Accessed 11/22/14.

What might explain these poor giving patterns? One explanation might be that many Christians do not know that their wealth truly belongs to God or that they should be generous with their giving. However, we suspect that is not the case; even a cursory reading of the Bible and occasional church attendance would quickly provide a sufficient education to anyone who might be confused about where God stands on the topics of wealth and money. A second explanation is that many Christians know their wealth truly belongs to God and that they should be generous with their giving, but they do not know how to actually implement those behaviors in practice. The barriers to obedience in these areas is likely a combination of lack of knowledge about how to give, excessive worry about providing for one's family and saving for the future, and frankly, significant sin issues around selfishness, materialism, and lack of compassion for the poor. A major driver of these sin issues is the cultural context in which we live. Our consumerist culture, preaching materialism from every loudspeaker, likely shrouds these sin issues from many individuals. In *The Joy of the Gospel*, Pope Francis explains the outcome of this situation:

> *Almost without being aware of it, we end up being incapable of feeling compassion at the outcry of the poor, weeping for other people's pain, and feeling a need to help them, as though all this were someone else's responsibility and not our own. The culture of prosperity deadens us; we are thrilled if the market offers us something new to purchase. In the meantime all those lives stunted for lack of opportunity seem a mere spectacle; they fail to move us.*[94]

Many of us are probably unaware of the extent to which we have been influenced by our culture to become more attached to our

---

94 Pope Francis. *The Joy of the Gospel*, 46.

wealth and less grateful to God for His provision and blessing, even as many of us suffer from a "bad conscience" around our material wealth and giving—a "slight itch" that tells us we should be doing more. Overall, this is a depressing situation. With the picture looking so bleak, we began to wonder if there is any hope on the horizon. Are there pockets within the Church where giving is more prevalent, and if so, what can we learn from these hopeful anomalies?

A first whiff of hopefulness can be found in the Science of Generosity data set presented in the book *Passing the Plate*.[95] We have seen that most Americans are not generous, including many professing Christians. However, what if we narrowed in on regular church-attending Christians who earn more than $90,000 per year? Theoretically, this group contains Christians who are at least semi-devoted (enough to get up on Sunday morning and go to church) and also have the clear financial capacity to give. Encouragingly, this demographic gives an average of 8.8 percent of gross income away each year, a significantly higher number.

Perhaps it is unrealistic to survey self-identified Christians across America and expect to see anything materially different from our society at large. This is a nation that has been a culturally Christian nation in the past, where people may simply claim the religious affiliation without actually knowing much about the person of Jesus Christ. Billy Graham famously estimated that only 25 percent of church attendees are truly born-again Christians. According to the data in *Passing the Plate*, the most generous 25 percent of church members give 90 percent of total funds taken in by the church in America. (Note that this is the most generous 25 percent as sorted by percent-of-income-given, not sorted by total amount given. So the figure includes a person giving a big

---

95 Christian Smith and Michael Emerson, *Passing the Plate*, Oxford University Press, 2008, 47.

fraction of their $10,000 income, but excludes the person earning one million dollars who gives two percent of it to the church.) With this single anecdote, it becomes interesting to speculate on whether moving closer to Christ and His church is a causal driver of greater generosity.

To investigate this possibility, we set out on an informal research project of our own. What if we could go one level deeper, and seek out highly devoted followers of Jesus who earn very high incomes? What would we find? Our survey on Christian Wealth and Giving, conducted in the fall of 2014, gave some preliminary answers to this question, and we were astonished and encouraged by the results.

Table 4: Charitable Giving Rates by Various Demographics

Demographic	Giving Rate
Americans	<3%
Wealthy Americans	<3%
"Christian" Americans	<3%
Churchgoing Christian Americans	5-8%
Informal Survey of Wealthy, Devoted Christians	>10%

Notice the progression. As you zero-in and select for devotion and the presence of disposable income, the level of giving dramatically increases.

One of our good friends at Harvard Business School, who is from Liberia, another largely Christian nation, made a cultural observation that we believe is relevant here. Different cultures have different areas of sin that are normalized and accepted, whereas other areas of sin get aggressively called out. All sin is worthy of attention, but the culture one resides within will dictate just how serious certain transgressions appear in the public eye. In

America, certain sexual sins are really a big deal, as they should be. But financial greed is not condemned very loudly. In fact, it is at times a virtue! No one will be ostracized in America because of their financial stinginess.

In Liberia, things are just the opposite. While there is a certain sexual permissiveness in the Liberian culture, a lack of generosity is met with complete social disdain. It is seen as unacceptable to become wealthy without sharing one's abundance with others. We need to try and be aware of our cultural blinders. In a consumerist society that celebrates wealth and individualism, we must be careful to avoid succumbing to numbness toward the sin of financial miserliness.

THE GENEROSITY OF DEVOTED CHRISTIAN BUSINESS LEADERS

"I am basically trying to die 'broke'. I want to give it all away while I am alive to ensure it gets to the right places that I intended. Giving for me is a form of worship and a test of my heart – is my heart in money/stuff or is my heart for God? Materialism is nothing more than a distraction and a barrier to a growing faith."

—Survey Response

Our survey included over 200 individuals and had two primary objectives. First, we sought to understand how higher-income Christians think about and manage their wealth and giving today. Second, we hoped to test the attractiveness of the ideas we were exploring for this book. Here is a summary of the key insights generated by the survey.

SURVEY RESPONDENT DEMOGRAPHICS

All of the survey respondents identify as Christian, and 99 percent state that their faith is "very important" or "central" to how they live their lives. The majority of respondents are Harvard Business School alumni; other respondents include personal and professional contacts of both the authors and the survey respondents themselves (we asked that the HBS alumni to whom we sent the survey forward it to other individuals in their networks who would be a good candidate to take the survey).[96] Ages ranged from people in their twenties to those in their seventies, and wealth ranged from middle class to those with $20 million or more. The median or prototypical survey-taker is a male in his forties, who lives in a household with three or four people, attends a non-denominational church, earns $200,000 to $400,000 per year, and has a net worth of $1 million to $5 million.

CHRISTIAN GIVING

"Ten percent of a million is not really sacrificing much.
I believe the percentage should grow as income grows."
—Survey Response

We first hoped to understand how higher-income Christians think about and actually manage their wealth and giving today. What we learned is that most higher-income Christians (approximately 60 percent) believe they should give the "traditional tithe" (i.e., 10 percent of income) plus additional offerings as led by God. Only approximately 10 percent of respondents believe Christians are called to give "only" the traditional tithe. The remaining approximately 20 percent believe Christians should give whatever portion of their income they feel called to give. Our respondents

---

96 Because the survey is anonymous, we do not know the exact mix of respondents between HBS alumni and non-HBS alumni.

appear to be putting their money where their mouths are: the median respondent gives 10 percent of household income each year, with some giving 20 percent or more.

TESTING LIFESTYLE LIMIT AND NET WORTH LIMIT

> *"I have been giving 50 percent of our income since we reached a few million dollars in net worth, more than a decade ago. . . . We give away almost all if not more than all of our current income, but assets have continued to appreciate."*
>
> —Survey Response

After understanding how our survey respondents manage their wealth and giving today, we tested the attractiveness of intentionally limiting one's lifestyle in order to give more generously, specifically by either limiting annual spending or net worth. We asked about respondents' interest in the idea, as well as what dollar figure they might consider for such limits. This latter question is obviously very dependent upon an individual's specific circumstances, including geography, number of children, obligation to care for elderly parents or children with special needs, etc. However, it is still instructive to see where survey respondents think these limits should be, on average.

Table 5: Survey Takers' Suggestion for a Reasonable Lifestyle Spending Limit

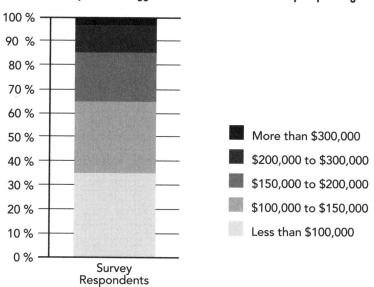

Just over 50 percent of respondents react positively to spending limits, with the majority placing the value of such a limit at less than $150,000 per year. More striking is the response to our question about net worth limits. Roughly a quarter of respondents said they do this or plan to, and another quarter said they did not like the idea. *More than half,* however, reported that they found the idea intriguing, but had either never heard it or had never given it much thought. The idea of discovering "how much is enough" is not new, especially in Christian circles, so we find it fascinating that over half of a large sample of business leaders had never wrestled with it! Part of our hope for this book is that more people will be exposed to this idea. The median net worth limit suggested was around $5 million, with half suggesting a higher number, and half a lower number.

Table 6: What Do You Believe this Net Worth Limit Should Be for Your Family? (# of Respondents)

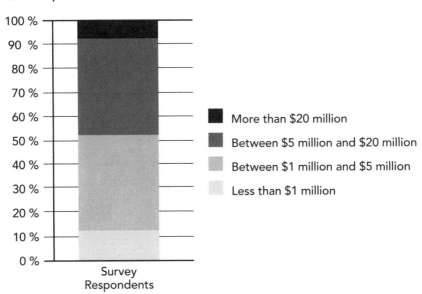

Legend:
- More than $20 million
- Between $5 million and $20 million
- Between $1 million and $5 million
- Less than $1 million

X-axis: Survey Respondents

SUMMARY

The majority of respondents give 10 percent of income or more each year. Given that only three percent of Americans give 10 percent or more, it is striking that over 50 percent of this population does so. Survey-takers were split roughly evenly in terms of their support for the notion of a lifestyle spending limit. Support for a wealth limit was much higher, with 75 percent finding the idea favorable. That said, the gap between interest in and implementation of each concept highlights the need for greater education and communication about these topics in churches today—both the theological/scriptural basis for handling our wealth in this way, as well as practical education on how to actually execute these concepts in the real world (stay tuned for Chapters Five through Eight!). We are incredibly grateful to all

200-plus survey respondents, as well as those who helped us reach this audience.[97, 98]

THE COMPETITIVE CASE FOR GENEROSITY

In the faith community and in society at large, people are getting more and more excited about giving. The Christian case is emblematic: Fifteen years ago, there were two Christian stewardship ministries. Today, there are at least sixteen.[99] We are witnessing a proliferation of interest in the topic of how Christians should handle wealth for the glory of God.

Generous Giving is one of the oldest of those ministries and exists to grow generosity in the Body of Christ, especially among those of higher means. Todd Harper, the President of Generous Giving, has seen this momentum building over the last several years and offers a vision of where it could be heading:

> *What if the prevailing culture of Christian giving could change, such that it was no longer a rare exception to see someone living with radical financial generosity? What if hearing about Christians giving 50, 70, 90 percent away for the Kingdom was commonplace? What if the Christian who saved all of their money and accumulated a fortune was the anomaly, because everyone else was so focused on giving?*

---

97 In particular, we thank Jeff Barneson, Harvard University chaplain and leader of InterVarsity at Harvard Business School. Jeff allowed us access to his HBS alumni email list, which enabled us to reach such a wide audience of HBS alumni. We are also grateful to the many individuals who forwarded the survey to others in their networks.

98 We were greatly encouraged by the very high response rate. We believe this demonstrates both the strength of the HBS network (especially the HBS Christian Fellowship) and the importance of these topics in the lives of Christians around the globe.

99 Conversation with industry insider, who provided us with a strategic mapping of all the generosity/stewardship players along with the various ways in which they serve the Body of Christ.

For years and years, United States oil production continued to slowly decline. People felt that breaking through and reducing our dependence on foreign oil was impossible. But a few years ago, creative engineers and entrepreneurs discovered hydraulic fracturing, and everything changed. Nationally, production is up 50 percent. Geologists knew the resource was there—they just had not figured out how to get it. I believe Christian giving is in the same place. We as a Church are in the midst of figuring out how to begin releasing our tremendous wealth, which has been locked up within families, and begin mobilizing it to accomplish great works for the glory of God. The giving rate, which has been flat for so long, could start moving up, just as our oil production reversed a decades-old trend.

We believe that such a cultural change is within view, out on the horizon, if higher-income Christians awaken and take up the call to action. We want to be part of this! In fact, given the massive level of wealth present in American society today, we believe that such a cultural shift could enable the Church to finish the proclamation component of the Great Commission on a very short timescale.[100] When looking at the accumulation of wealth in human history, the trillions of dollars that exist today were mostly generated in just a few short generations. For all of human history until the Industrial Revolution of the 1700s, wealth was extremely limited. Today, global wealth stands in the tens of trillions of dollars. The "problem" of excess wealth, which used to be limited to kings, is

---

100 The Great Commission includes discipleship, which cannot be "finished." However, we yearn for the day when all people on earth have heard and had a chance to respond to the Gospel message of Jesus.

today applicable to millions of families. If the Christian Church were to activate and mobilize the colossal wealth resource that the Lord has entrusted it with, the results would be staggering.

Just to dream big for a moment, what do you think the price tag would be to accomplish all of the following? How sacrificially would we have to give to make these goals happen?

- Sponsor one million indigenous full-time missionaries in poor nations around the world

- Provide full resources for the global malaria campaign

- Quadruple the global missions budget for reaching unevangelized nations

- Provide food, clothing, and shelter to all 6.5 million refugees across Africa, Asia, and the Middle East

- Triple the global Bible translation budget

- Fund 150,000 seminary scholarships for promising students in emerging economies

- Double the operating budget of World Vision

- Establish eight new Christian universities around the world

- Hire 25,000 additional American missionaries to work on our college campuses

Does this seem impossibly ambitious? The price tag is $20 billion.[101] American Christians possess at their disposal an annual income of over $5 trillion,[102] making us the wealthiest community

---

101 Adapted from data in Christian Smith and Michael Emerson, *Passing the Plate*, Oxford University Press, 2008. We are grateful for the incredibly compelling work these authors present in Chapter One of their book on this topic.

102 Stearns, *The Hole in Our Gospel*

of believers in world history. If we collectively spent 0.4 percent of our income, or one dollar out of $250, we could achieve the goals laid out here. We believe that God has ordained the modern era of history for wealth creation, and that the heavy responsibility of managing the windfall is distributed across millions of well-off Christians in the Western world.

Given the massive level of wealth in the hands of modern humans, it would make sense for giving movements to begin springing up, and for Christians to be leading the charge. This has in fact begun—VMWare CEO Pat Gelsinger, a Christian, recently appeared in *Business Insider* in a piece highlighting that he gives away half of his income, motivated by his strong Christian faith.[103] However, we have also noticed that a majority of articles about generosity highlight secular movements.

- Bill Gates' Giving Pledge has been signed by 128 billionaire families, who have all committed to give away at least half of their net worth during their lifetimes, or upon their death.

- For those with fewer resources, Peter Singer has organized a Pledge associated with his book *The Life You Can Save*. This pledge requires a minimum commitment of giving one percent of income toward highly effective organizations fighting extreme poverty around the globe.

- There is also Giving What We Can, which has a higher bar for its pledge. Members must sign and commit to give at least 10 percent of income for life, from the time of signing until retirement, to alleviating global suffering. Note that this organization has no religious affiliation whatsoever, yet its standards for giving are higher than that of most American

---

103 "The CEO of this $30 billion company gives half of his gross income to charity," *Business Insider*, http://www.businessinsider.com/this-ceo-gives-away-half-of-his-income-2015-8, accessed September, 2015.

churches! Despite being just a few years old, the organization has accumulated over $100 million in pledges.

- Finally, there is a group called Radical Givers, whose members pledge at least 33 percent of their gross income to highly effective global charities in order to fight extreme poverty.

None of these pledges has a Christian orientation, yet each has driven powerful results around the world for the benefit of "the least of these." We would love to see Christians begin to out-do these efforts with pledges and movements of our own. We believe that the Church should be leading the conversation around global giving, and out-pledging the pledgers we see in society today. While Christians today do in fact give quite a bit to mission work and poverty alleviation, couldn't we begin to raise the bar higher?

In the next few chapters, we'll zoom in from the macro perspective we have been taking and step into a deep study of how our money can be used on a personal level. In "Part II: Frameworks," we ask ourselves hard and honest questions about consumption, saving, and giving, striving to uncover the most life-giving way that each incremental dollar can be used in our lives.

PART II: FRAMEWORKS

CHAPTER FIVE

The "Three S Framework:"
Spender, Saver, or Servant?

*"Make no mistake about it. Ideas matter. The ideas
one really believes largely determine the kind of person
one becomes. Everyone has a philosophy of life. That
is not optional. What is optional and, thus, of extreme
importance is the adequacy of one's philosophy of life."*

—J. P. Moreland and William Lane Craig

In Part I, we attempted to make three key points. First, the
Christian tradition has quite a lot to say about giving, which
is backed up by evidence from both secular philosophy and the
social sciences. Second, today's Christians, despite living in the
wealthiest society in history, give a relatively small portion of
their resources to advance Christ's Church and to help the poor.
Third, there are some notable exceptions to this troubling gap—
Christians who sacrificially submit their financial resources to
God in profound and even shocking ways. As we contemplated
these realities, we wondered whether there is a common frame

of mind that differentiates highly generous Christians, including our case studies, from the rest of American Christians. And also, given the biblical principles laid out in Part I, would it be possible to capture the worldview of these generous individuals, translating it into a practical and actionable giving plan that any 21st-century believer can follow and work toward?

We believe the answer to both questions is a resounding yes. After studying this issue deeply, we believe that someone's mindset of money will tend toward one of three possibilities. Your "money mindset" will make you a Spender, a Saver, or a Servant with your financial resources.

- A **Spender**, represented by most people in the Western world, is someone who pursues the greatest possible present consumption, even if mindful of the need to save some.

- A **Saver**, by contrast, strives to limit consumption to some extent, focusing instead on increased wealth accumulation.

- A **Servant**, possessing the rarest mindset of all, orients their life around limiting both consumption and wealth-building, focusing instead on giving the most money they can toward blessing other people.

Your money mindset is driven by two factors: your temporal focus and your view on the highest purpose of money. Temporally, Spenders maximize value today, Savers maximize value in the future, and Servants maximize value in eternity. These attitudes are driven by your view of money's purpose. A Spender views financial resources as a way to "live it up," enjoying every part of the high life that money can buy. Savers have a more complex view of money, viewing it mostly as a tool for security, stability, flexibility, and personal freedom or agency. A Saver's net worth might become a simple way to "keep score" in life. Servants, by contrast, view their money as a potential blessing to the world in Christ's name, desiring to make the most of its potential for positive impact.

The three money mindsets definitely bleed into one another, but each of us can identify our own core mindset by looking at the highest hopes we have for our wealth. Rather than just examining the percent of income spent, saved, or given, it is better to ask, "Where would I focus my thoughts and efforts if my income began dramatically increasing over time?" If you would spend, spend, and spend some more to enjoy all that the world has to offer, you are (you guessed it) a Spender. If you would seek to pay off the mortgage early, retire early, or build a family dynasty of wealth, perhaps you're a Saver. If you would immediately begin thinking about how to give your excess resources to Christian initiatives around the world, you're definitely a Servant.

I (John) was a card-carrying Saver before beginning this project, and am slowly and prayerfully trying to make the transition to Servant. I wanted to retire as soon as possible, build a lasting family dynasty by making my children wealthy, and eventually reach a seven or eight-figure net worth to ensure stability of lifestyle. As I mentioned in the Preface, my internet password was literally "Retire_at_40!" Every time I logged into a bank or brokerage online, I was reminded of my singular focus on obtaining financial independence. Greg, on the other hand, reflects on being a Spender before we began this project together. While he did set aside moderate funds for tithing and retirement savings, he viewed the remaining funds as fair game for spending on whatever seemed fun at the time. With a monthly budget for dining out of $1,000, and annual travel expenses of over $5,000, he strove to live life to the fullest and maximize the enjoyment he could get out of his high earning power. Even though Greg and I both tithed off our incomes, we were not Servants. I viewed my tithe as a mildly bothersome requirement that prevented me from building wealth faster. Greg thought tithing would help him "stay in God's good graces" so he could otherwise spend as he pleased. We each felt good about our "faithful giving," but neither of us had the right money mindset.

SELF-DIAGNOSIS

So where do you stack up? Take the following quiz, circling the answer that most closely aligns with your heart. This is meant to be a light-hearted and non-scientific exercise, so don't feel any pressure. We'll give away the answer key up front—*A* corresponds to a Spender, *B* corresponds to a Saver, and *C* corresponds to a Servant. Our guess is that 99 percent of the population, when being honest, will circle mostly *A*s or *B*s. Even after our journey, John gravitates toward the Saver answers, and Greg toward the Spender ones, but we are continually striving to grow the heart of a Servant! Give it a try:

1. What excites you more?

    A. A four-star vacation across Europe.

    B. Maxing out all retirement accounts for the year.

    C. Dinner with your pastor, who expresses heartfelt thanks for your sacrificial support of a successfully launched, new, key ministry.

2. What was your tendency as a child, with regard to new money you received?

    A. To buy new toys or spend on experiences as soon as you got it.

    B. To save it in a piggy bank or savings account.

    C. To spend on or give to others, your church, or charities.

3. You hear about a man who, at 70, has managed his middle-class income through careful savings, with a current net worth of eight million dollars. Your first thought is:

   A. What a waste! Spending it would have been more fun!

   B. Wow, he really did well. I hope I can do that, too.

   C. He may have missed some opportunities to experience the joy of generosity.

4. Success looks like . . .

   A. Experiencing great food and travel, hosting friends, driving a luxury car.

   B. Retiring at 50.

   C. Lengthening home payoff and forgoing some luxuries in order to sponsor a missionary family.

5. Your annual bonus is twice as much as you thought it would be. What do you first think?

   A. I'm headed out shopping/on vacation.

   B. I'm putting this on the mortgage.

   C. Thank God for this provision. I can't wait to give a chunk of this away.

6. The spending in my life is:

   A. Effortless—I love it.

   B. Bothersome—I wish I could spend less.

   C. Controlled—I feel good about the way it's managed.

7. The saving in my life is:

   A. Bothersome—It's an inconvenience that gets in the way of having fun.

   B. Effortless—I love building wealth.

   C. Purposeful—I have healthy and reasonable goals toward which I'm carefully working.

8. The giving in my life is:

    A. Obligatory.

    B. Formulaic.

    C. Joyfully overflowing.

Tally up your score! The more your answers lean toward the same letter each time, the more you have a clue as to how your heart inclines. If you're married, it may be worthwhile to see where your spouse falls and compare answers—and this may provoke an interesting conversation highlighting where money conflicts may have originated. There's nothing wrong with having opposing money mindsets, but knowing that this is the case may be helpful in praying and working through the need for alignment on money issues in a marriage relationship. Working together toward becoming Christian Servants can be a unifying pursuit.

Christian Spenders and Savers often cast judgment on those with the opposite mindset in a subtle, subconscious way. If I had known Greg before we met at Harvard, I would have said something to my wife Megan like, "Look at this joker. Why is he spending all his money? They have some awesome vacations and even drop $80 for dinner dates, but his savings rate is pathetically low. We'll see who was smart when we're retired in 20 years and he's still working."

Meanwhile, Greg might have been thinking, "Why does John not spend any money? He's such a miser. He never takes his wife on trips or out to nice restaurants. We could all die tomorrow! He needs to learn to enjoy himself a little!" These criticisms, we have realized, miss the point entirely.

Both Greg and his wife Alison, along with me and my wife Megan, were all entering our mid twenties, earning six figure incomes, and had plenty of "extra" to put toward Kingdom work—if we had been excited about doing so. The highest purpose of wealth, like the highest purpose of our lives, ought not to be enjoying today or finding security for tomorrow. Instead, the purpose of wealth should be to help us glorify God and enjoy Him forever! Servants know that they need things today, and they also realize that someday they may need to retire, send children to college, etc. However, their primary aim and focus is to serve Jesus with their money, and this means their decisions may appear anomalous to both Spenders and Savers.

Modern personal finance teaching tends to reside somewhere between spending and saving as well, while failing to recognize the "third axis" of Servanthood. Our cultural milieu views wealth-building as a centrally important and praiseworthy activity, and capitalism is built upon the central urge within the human heart to acquire more and more.[104] Most people who view themselves as mature when it comes to money are Savers, proudly basking in their own wealth-accumulation prowess (I, John, am talking about myself here!). Influential personalities such as Dave Ramsey encourage people to follow ratios with their money in the spirit of saving, with the ultimate aim of increasing wealth.[105] Giving generously is encouraged perhaps as one component of an overall plan, but building God's Kingdom here on Earth is not held up very clearly as the central purpose of money. Family legacies and the personal freedom that comes with wealth seem to be the

---

104 Adam Smith reflected on this driving behavior behind the capitalist system, and the emptiness that blind pursuit of wealth results in: "Through the whole of his life [the wealth-builder] pursues the idea of a certain artificial and elegant repose which he may never arrive at, for which he sacrifices a real tranquility that is at all times in his power. . . . (He) begins at last to find that wealth and greatness are mere trinkets of frivolous utility." Adam Smith, "Theory of Moral Sentiments," (1759, 1981, IV, I, 260-261).

105 In his latest book The Legacy Journey, Mr. Ramsey refers to accumulating wealth as "winning" (pages 13, 59) and explains how he convinced an NFL player that spending $100,000 per year was too little, and that the player should instead spend over $800,000 per year on himself instead of giving more aggressively (pages 80–82). Mr. Ramsey also refers to the moment when he purchased a Jaguar automobile, taking a moment to"[think] about all the hungry children in the world," but then postulates that God was smiling down on him as he wrote the check (page 3). He even argues that one's own children can probably manage money better than a charity you might donate toward. There is some valuable teaching present in the book, but these authors also found much to take issue with from a biblical perspective.

central goals instead. While we are indeed free as Christians, we are only free for the purpose of becoming servants of Christ.[106] We want to challenge the prevailing modern framework for thinking about money's purpose in life.

THINKING LIKE A SERVANT

Ron Blue, a pioneer of Christian financial advising, tells the story of a couple he was helping that made $85,000 per year. He challenged them to give away one million dollars in their lifetimes—and they thought he was crazy! But they couldn't shake the thought. When Ron ran into them decades later, they excitedly told him that they had indeed given one million dollars away . . . three times! It had become much more fun to track cumulative giving than to track net worth. When their mindset flipped and they latched onto a goal, they began giving much more aggressively.

The next few chapters have the goal of articulating how a Servant thinks about Spending, Saving, and Serving. None of our specific recommendations are intended to be legalistically binding—we do not want to become Pharisees by adding to the law. Rather, they are simply our method for working out the implications of Scripture in a practical way, based on what we've seen working in the lives of our case studies. There may be other great ways to walk out life as a well-off Christian, but this is our best stab at it.

While we do acknowledge that there is room for disagreement on the tactics of being a Servant, we want to stand firm and say that all faithful Christians *must be Servants* in order to live a life that is consistent with Scripture. We cannot claim to live fully in accordance with God's word if we let the mindset of a Spender or Saver drive our actions! To reiterate, Servants will necessarily

---

106 1 Peter 2:16, paraphrase.

spend money on themselves and save money for future needs, but only insofar as doing so brings honor and glory to God. The ultimate aim of a Servant's wealth must be the glory of God, consistent with Scripture, not present enjoyment or future wealth accumulation.

To demonstrate the insufficiency of the Saver mindset encouraged by modern personal finance teaching, we present a paraphrase of the Parable of the Rich Fool, in which we replace ancient symbols of wealth with modern ones.

> *Someone in the crowd said to him, "Teacher, tell my boss to pay the full year-end performance bonus he promised me."*
>
> *But he said to him, "Man, who made me a judge or arbitrator over you?" And he said to them, "Take care, and be on your guard against all covetousness, for one's life does not consist in the abundance of his possessions." And he told them a parable, saying, "The stock options belonging to a manager vested after a major run-up in share price, and he thought to himself, 'What shall I do, for I already have enough saved to send my kids to college, my house is paid off, and I already max out my 401k every year!' And he said, 'I will do this: I will open an investment account and create a passive income portfolio, and I'll exercise my options and put the money there. And I will say to my soul, "Soul, you have a big enough portfolio to be financially independent; retire early, plan some vacations, play golf."'*

But God said to him, 'Fool! This night your soul is required of you, and the portfolio you've built, what use will it be then?' So is the one who endlessly builds his net worth and is not rich toward God." [107]

The Rich Fool is someone who puts their hope for security and comfort in riches, rather than in the God who has generously provided them. The Rich Fool is someone who finds their personal worth wrapped up in their net worth. John was in the process of becoming a rich fool when we began this project. [108]

A Spender mindset, with its focus on material things, is also called out in Scripture. In the Parable of the Sower, Jesus explains how there are four types of people who hear His words. The first type don't understand, and the second type fall away when tested with trials. The fourth type is the type of soil Jesus is looking for— people who receive Him with joy and multiply their impact 30, 60, or 100 times. Don't we all want the hundredfold life? However, the Spender mindset could condemn us to become the third type of soil. Jesus describes the third type: "As for what was sown among thorns, this is the one who hears the word, but the cares of the world and the deceitfulness of riches choke the word, and it proves unfruitful" (Matthew 13:22). Did you catch that? Basically, Jesus is saying, "Some of you will hear my words, but you'll be . . . distracted, chasing the Joneses. I'll get crowded out by financial matters, and you won't bear any fruit." Greg was in the process of becoming the third soil when our journey began, but has now begun choosing Jesus more than the Joneses.

---

107 Author's paraphrase of the Parable of the Rich Fool, from Luke 12.

108 The Rich Fool's entire net worth, according to our best estimate, was probably a few hundred thousand dollars. According to Thomas Piketty's *Capital in the Twenty-First Century*, wealthy nobility of the ancient world typically had incomes 20 to 30 times greater than that of a laborer, earned through capital ownership, at approximately a five percent rate of return. Given the modest incomes of laborers in the ancient near east, this puts the Rich Fool's income around $10,000 to $20,000 per year, and his net worth at $200,000 to $400,000. I am humbled that my suburban, four-bedroom home might be worth more than the entire estate of the Rich Fool.

Jesus points out the fatal flaws we can exhibit toward money through being either Savers or Spenders with these parables. If our mindset leads us to believe we can become secure and fulfilled through increasing wealth, He calls us fools. If our mindset leads us to become distracted by the pursuits made possible by our money—thinking that happiness is just one purchase away—He calls us unfruitful. Either way, we miss the mark. Saver John and Spender Greg invite you to come along as we look at how Servants can more fruitfully live lives for Christ.

Before moving forward and pushing into our framework, we want to acknowledge that every circumstance is unique, and exceptions are always bountiful. However, there are sufficient commonalities in modern life for us to draw some useful and generalized conclusions about personal finance.

The framework that follows represents our attempt to build a practical, actionable wealth and giving guide for a modern Christian that is based on the three money mindsets. We are conscious that there are always nuances, exceptional cases, and complicating factors, and we have done our best to incorporate them. For whatever we have missed, the principles of Scripture can guide the incorporation of further complexities for each person's individual circumstances. The system we propose is aggressive relative to current giving trends in the Church. We believe this aggressiveness reflects the true call of Jesus to His followers. It combines a modern understanding of personal finance and wealth planning with the ancient truths and exhortations of the Christian faith, all with the goal of giving believers a way to think systematically about their role as wealth stewards on the Earth.

THE MONEY MAP

God has delegated to us the absolute earthly control (stewardship) over how we allocate the financial resources that come to us. These resources ultimately belong to God, however. So our high degree of control comes with great responsibility. Our desire is to present tools to help address the multiple allocation decisions that a person will be faced with. The first allocation decision is related to consumption: "How much of my income should be kept for spending?" The second is related to wealth accumulation: "Considering the funds I have not spent, how much should I give, and how much should I save?"[109] These are the two primary questions on which our analysis is built.

Figure 1: The Wealth-Allocation Decision: Three Money Mindsets

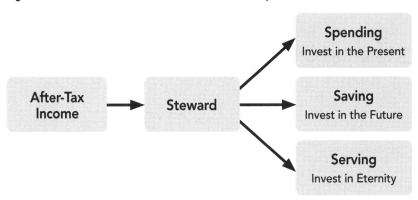

109 We recognize that Christian teaching often focuses on giving first fruits to the Lord, then consuming from what is left. We agree with and endorse such a mindset. However, we believe starting with consumption cuts more quickly to the heart of where financial problems originate in our culture of consumerism. In day-to-day life, we believe giving should indeed come first. As seen in the previous chapter, giving is an activity of critical importance for all people. In the mode of thinking presented in our framework, however, we want to begin by carefully evaluating the consumption decision, which will then allow for generous giving to develop in a more holistic way.

We explore each *S*—Spending, Saving, and Serving—in the following three chapters. Before diving in, we present a diagram below that we believe represents how a Servant views the difficult decision of allocating financial resources. This is the way the Servants we have studied view the world of money. (Readers who have been through business school, or who have worked with management consultants, will quickly recognize this as a 2x2 matrix. It would be tragic for two Harvard MBAs to write a book without a 2x2, so here it is in Figure 2: The Servant's Money Map.)

Figure 2: The Servant's Money Map

Are Saving Needs Met?

"I have plenty of wealth"

Zone 3

Give A Lot

No Saving

Personal Wealth Finish Line

Zone 4

Give Radically

No Saving

"I could use some more wealth"

Zone 1

Give Some

Save Some

Spending Finish Line

Zone 2

Give A Lot

Save A Lot

"I could use some more income"

"I make plenty of income"

Are Spending Needs Met?

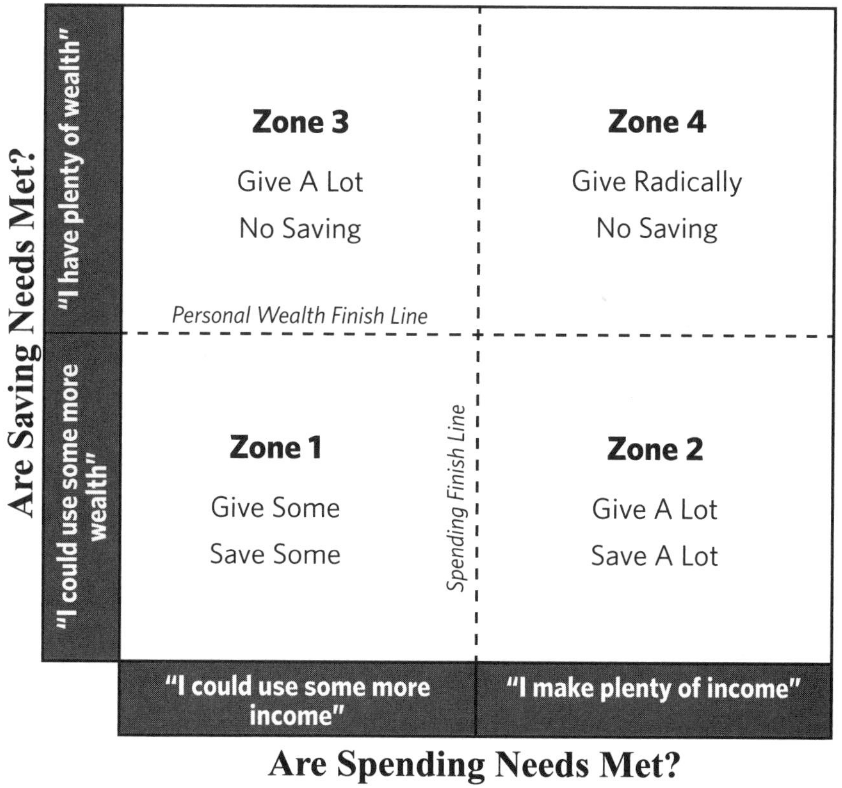

Each zone on the diagram above represents a possible state of the world for a Servant. The four zones are delineated by the Servant's spending needs and saving needs. In spending, if a Servant feels that their family's legitimate needs and healthy desires are not being fully met by their income, they fall on the left hand side: "I could use some more income." If they feel well-provided for and that their income is plentiful, they fall on the right: "I make plenty of income." In Saving, the same logic holds for net worth. If the family has a mortgage to pay, retirement to save for, etc., they probably feel that they "could use some more wealth." If they have all their wealth needs taken care of, they "have plenty of wealth."

- **Zone 1** represents a situation in which the Servant has a need for more income and wealth. Giving and saving are both fundamentally important, so they'll strive to do a bit of each, but it will require some effort and planning to be successful.

- In **Zone 2**, income is sufficient, but wealth-building is still needed. Balanced giving and saving occurs in this zone for a faithful Servant.

- In **Zone 3**, high wealth is mixed with low income (think wealthy retiree or entrepreneur with illiquid wealth). There is no need to save, but the ability to give is hampered by liquidity constraints.

- In **Zone 4**, all financial needs have been met, enabling the Servant to give with extraordinary freedom.

Zone 1 is where most people start and live a large portion of their lives. With student loans to pay and entry-level salaries, most people could certainly use a little more income and wealth in their lives. There is nothing unholy about this, and Servants recognize their own needs for provision.

Whatever zone they reside in, however, Servants eagerly anticipate the day when they might reach Zone 4, beginning a journey of extravagant giving enabled by their understanding that God has given them financial sufficiency in their own life. Their highest aim, rather than accumulating more wealth or increasing their lifestyle, is to give to God's work.

Spenders will never reach Zone 4—to them it does not exist. They have no conception of "I make plenty of income," because incremental earnings can always find a way to get spent. Savers will never get to Zone 4, either, because "I could use some more wealth" is effectively their heart's rallying cry, whether they have amassed one thousand dollars or one million. For the Servant, however, financial life is a careful navigation toward a clear goal: bringing God glory with the wealth He provides.

Some Servants live their entire lives in Zone 1. There is nothing wrong with this outcome from what we have learned in reading Scripture. For the Servant who lives responsibly but is not in a position to build significant wealth or earn a high income, it is important to remember that net worth is not personal worth. In God's eyes, the faithful giving of five percent, ten percent, or fifteen percent of income that someone in Zone 1 executes consistently may be more valuable than the fifty percent giving rate of another Servant who was blessed to reach Zone 4. We are in no position to make such a judgment. Such giving is certainly more valuable to God than the wrongly motivated tithes that Greg and I gave prior to business school (when we were in Zone 2). The mindset, not the money, is what God is most interested in.

For now, imagine which zone you might currently reside in, and think about the implications of this for your own stewardship. John, having taken a job in ministry after graduation and modestly cracking "six-figure income" territory, is living in Zone 1 right now. Driving older vehicles, purchasing a home in the suburbs rather than in a hot intown neighborhood, and buying furniture primarily at IKEA®, enable his family to save and give while enjoying God's provision in this stage of life. Greg has a fantastic income close to $200,000 (and some upside for large bonuses), but also a pile of student loans and a growing family. All of which mean that he's in Zone 2, giving generously while also saving to meet his family's legitimate needs. We each are striving to balance giving and saving, trusting in the Lord, while providing well for our families.

In upcoming chapters we will investigate how to more specifically think about establishing the cutoff points for each zone boundary, the "Finish Lines" labeled in the Servant's Money Map. With this framework in mind, we will turn to the first major decision a Servant must make: how much to spend.

For a Closer Look . . .

Straight out of college, Graham Smith went to Wall Street with plans to give 90 percent of his income away—totally in service to Jesus. He wanted to live in Zone 4 from day one! He met his wife April in the city, a recent MBA grad with a shared desire to give herself away for God's Kingdom. Check out their amazing story—a beautiful glimpse into the hearts of two Servants—in this seven-minute video "Graham and April Smith" at GodandMoney. net/resources.

CHAPTER SIX

Spending—Investing in the Present

*"And I commend joy, for man has nothing better under
the sun but to eat and drink and be joyful, for this will
go with him in his toil through the days of his life that
God has given him under the sun."*

—Ecclesiastes 8:15

*"Do you want to know the nine most disruptive words
in the Christian language? 'I have learned to be content
whatever the circumstances.'"*

—Jeff Manion

The first *S* we will investigate is Spending. Brett and Christy
Samuels, from Atlanta, Georgia, present an excellent case
study. In early 2012, they made a leap of faith. As newlyweds, the
Samuels had been enjoying great prosperity. Brett had landed a
job at a major management consulting firm after graduation and
was now earning well over $100,000 per year, while Christy was
adding another $22,000 on top of that in her role as a children's
minister at a local church. They seemed to be living up to their
own expectations for what a prosperous life should be. Growing

up, Brett's family had always earned enough money to not have a budget or worry about where each dollar went, and it felt good to be in the same boat now, despite being under 30 years old. Christy had inherited a deep nervousness around money from her own past, struggling with the scarcity mindset that can lead someone to become a Saver. Since they were socking away $5,000 per month into savings, their financial life seemed stable and predictable.

Until now, that is. Brett was about to leave his consulting job to start a company around some patents that his grandfather owned. The technologies were useful ones but had never been commercialized, and Brett was certain he was the man for the job. In taking on this new challenge, the Samuels would have to cut their budget dramatically. For an indefinite period of time, Brett would not earn a steady income as he built a new start-up enterprise. This left Christy's smaller paycheck as the only stable income. Making ends meet each month would no longer be automatic.

After prayerfully establishing what they described as a "life-giving" budget, the Samuels began their new journey. Realizing that they needed to cut their spending in half, their goal was to eliminate waste and increase the intentionality of their spending. They wanted their remaining spending to be biblically based, honoring to God, and to enable them to live life to the fullest. When we asked for an example, they pointed to haircuts. "How do you categorize having a professional stylist cut your hair? For us, that was a luxury that we could give up. For some people we know, that's a non-negotiable that falls under 'Personal Care.'" According to Christy, it is important to prioritize what really matters versus what feels necessary but truly isn't.

In 2012 and in 2013, Brett and Christy spent under $45,000, a dramatic reduction from their prior lifestyle. Reflecting on this, they both speak with the calm, steady confidence that comes only from experience. They come across as thoughtful and articulate, and their steady logic and passion to figure out how to honor God with their spending left us feeling deeply inspired.

Christy continued, "All spending should be life-giving from a biblical perspective, so we cut the consumer culture line items. It's not about the money; it's about the *consumption*. It's extra, too much. Our lives are not materially different, even though we're spending half what we used to. What's missing from our life? Random purchases from big box stores? It doesn't even hurt! The veil is lifted off your eyes, and you see the lie of, 'You need more! You need more!' When you realize you can make due with less, it shatters the lie. When you step out of it, you begin disliking the consumer culture."

The Samuels have experienced such freedom from this experience that they intend to continue living this way, even as their income increases in the future. Brett's start-up company has been doing well, but there is always uncertainty when running a new business. They see no reason to bump up their spending, even though it would be possible at this point. When we shared part of Denise Whitfield's story with the Samuels, they reflected that they had also experienced a shift from a scarcity mindset to an abundance mindset through being forced to cut their consumption. Brett states that "we do not want to become people who earn as much as we can and then just spend it willy-nilly."

Christy adds that "It's not as much about happiness as it is about holiness. We learned a lot about God's sovereignty, which was transformational to our worldview. Not being able to spend on extras at Target, or a margarita, etc., made me realize how little I actually needed those things."

The Samuels' new perspective on money was put to the test recently when they welcomed a baby girl into their family. Their

Servant mindset seemed to react to this new reality with sure-footedness, confidence, and maturity. Although their spending trend jumped from $45,000 per year toward $60,000 (mostly due to a fixed line item of $12,000 for childcare), their mindset remains the same. They do not feel the need to spend lavishly upon their child, despite having the growing ability to do so. "We need to understand that what is best for our daughter may not be more material prosperity. The Lord knows what she needs, and she is the Lord's more than she is ours. The best thing for her is not to live in a bubble of wealth."

This perspective, coming from a young couple, reminded us of a comment made by someone we met who has worked with many wealthy families in the past couple of decades—that the "best way to raise a child is broadly middle class, I'm saying roughly $50,000 to $250,000. There are problems that get bigger and harder to solve as you get outside of that range. Every wealthy family thinks they are the ones who can be different, but the reality is often disappointing."

SPENDING FRAMEWORK

The story of Brett and Christy Samuels is a good demonstration of how a family followed the core dictum of personal finance, to "Live beneath your means," in various seasons of life. Their great wisdom, however, is found in *how* they lived beneath their means—with joy, intentionality, and trust in the Lord. Needless to say, if we don't control our spending, saving and giving simply are not possible at any meaningful level.

A person who spends all of their income has no rainy day fund, will struggle to pay for their children's college or wedding expenses, cannot give generously, and may struggle to retire in old age. By contrast, a person who lives more frugally, diligently saving and giving, accumulates treasure in Heaven while also responsibly providing for their family here on Earth. A proper attitude toward consumption is therefore a prerequisite to a proper attitude toward giving. Without getting our mindset of spending right, we'll be forever hamstrung as givers. We have to overcome the Spender within to become Servants to Christ.

To think more deeply about spending, let's start at the low end. Lack of income creates obvious problems for spending, saving, and serving. It is extremely difficult to survive below an income level that affords basic provision. Below this level, the trade-offs required are gut-wrenching: food for dinner or medicine for your sick child? Indeed, a recent study even found that cash handouts for poor families could dramatically alter the course of a child's life for the better, permanently. For these families, spending is not about materialism, but rather basic provision and sustenance.[110] It is thus likely that many Christian working-class families fail to either save or give in great measure because they simply have no margin to do so.

Despite the clear fact that low-income families could easily spend their entire income on basic goods and services, allocating some income toward saving and giving remains a wise choice. Even those living on a dollar-per-day in third world nations often choose to wisely save a nickel or dime each day for emergencies or future capital outlays.[111] And similarly, our research into the sociology of giving has shown us that giving is critical for all people, including those of very modest means. As discussed in Chapter Three, giving activates human agency and creates the healthy set of mental processes that are associated with the abundance mindset.

---

110 National Bureau of Economic Research, http://www.nber.org/papers/w21562.pdf, accessed October, 2015

111 You can search the internet for "Rotating savings and credit associations" to learn how individuals in the poorest nations on earth still save, even without access to formal bank accounts.

Radical, faithful generosity and spending patterns are situational, and cannot be determined by simply looking at financial ratios. Perhaps a family earning $30,000 per year, pinching pennies in order to give five percent and save five percent, may be more faithful to the Gospel than someone like me, earning six figures before business school and tithing on autopilot, never really feeling the impact of my giving. Even though the lower-income family in this example gave a smaller portion, it might be "in keeping with their income," representing a real sacrifice of felt needs in order to give. If this family earned $40,000 in the next year, their gains could be mostly consumed, spent on safer housing, improved nutrition, school supplies, and other necessities, so any additional giving they choose to do is both wise and commendable from a biblical standpoint. Meanwhile, if I were to earn an extra $10,000 on my annual bonus and then give it all away, I wouldn't even miss it! Thus, the "pull" of spending is often dependent upon absolute income level. For this hypothetical family and millions of others throughout our society, marginal income tends to be mostly allocated toward the most pressing felt needs. Giving becomes a highly sacrificial act of love. (For a rich person to follow suit appears to be just as difficult as a camel making it through a needle's eye [Matthew 19:24].)

As a spending budget increases, then, higher-level needs begin to be addressed. At lower spending levels, wisely allocated dollars are immediately spent on physiological needs such as health care and food. In middle spending ranges, safety and stability take prominence. Taking center stage are goals such as improved housing, training or job advancement. As spending increases from there, human dignity and flourishing become the focus, with travel, education, and entertainment representing most of the marginal spending. Figure 3 is an attempt to roughly correlate various spending levels to Maslow's hierarchy of needs,[112] illustrating this principle for a family of four in a typical American city. This is not to suggest that all human needs can be met with money, but is rather indicative of the broad financial concerns of those in each budgetary bracket.[113]

Figure 3:
Mapping of Spending Budgets to Maslow's Hierarchy of Needs for American Family of Four

Self-Actualization, Belonging, Esteem
Spending power of $60,000 – $150,000
travel, entertainment, education, hobbies, relationships

Safety
Spending power of $25,000 – $60,000
improved housing, preventative health, insurance, lifestyle stability

Physiological Needs
Spending power below poverty line, less than $25,000
food, shelter, clothing, health emergencies

Clearly this is an oversimplification, but hopefully a helpful one. First of all, the numbers require adjustment for other family sizes. Also, some cities are more expensive than others—$150,000 in an average city equates to $135,000 in Nebraska, while it equates to $300,000 or more in San Francisco or New York City, based on cost of living differences.

---

112 Saul McLeod, "Maslow's Hierarchy of Needs," http://www.simplypsychology.org/maslow.html, accessed November, 2014.

113 The numbers chosen on this table are in 2016 dollars. For reference, $25,000 is the poverty line or roughly half the median family income of about $50,000. $150,000 is three times the median family income.

Overall, however, this chart serves to illustrate the relative ease or difficulty with which people choose to save or give their income, and a similar chart could be generated for each family's unique situation. For someone struggling to meet physiological needs, the decision to save or give rather than consume has huge personal ramifications. For the professional with a $150,000 budget, however, the decision to save or give may simply require a choice to forego the installation of a new swimming pool until next year. This is a much easier sacrifice to make. And for a fortunate few, the decision to save or give may simply come naturally, as their family spends all they reasonably desire and have plenty left over at the end of the year.

It is worth noting that Figure 3 has roots in well-established thinking from both the Christian and secular traditions. From the Christian angle, John Paul II writes of the distinction between "having" and "being" as these ideas relate to our spending patterns.[114] To have things has become a goal in itself in our consumeristic society, but this defies a Christian understanding of the world. Having possessions "does not in itself perfect the human subject, unless it contributes to the maturing and enrichment of that subject's 'being,' that is to say unless it contributes to the realization of the human vocation as such."[115] Maslow's hierarchy roughly corresponds to the wise spending of funds for human flourishing, whereas unwise spending characterized by conspicuous consumerism can result in emptiness.

We often witness a corruption of consumption patterns in both low- and high-income families—spending that focuses on "having" items that gratify human pride but does not enhance our ability to walk out our callings in life. Families of modest means might exceed wise spending levels to acquire a nice car, or make a habit of

114 Pope John Paul II, "Solicitudo Rei Socialis," (Rome, Italy), 1987.

115 Ibid.

unnecessarily splurging at the local mall on luxury branded items. This is a failure to consume wisely, which in turn hinders the ability to give or to save wisely. Similarly, more affluent families sometimes spend on their own versions of status symbols, such as a home in the nicest neighborhood in town or elite country club memberships, rather than using their funds to bless others through hospitality, experience the richness of the world through travel and culture, or enjoy shared experiences with friends and family. Both of these examples involve the use of material possessions to signal to others how prominent we are, an action that stems from haughtiness or self-importance. The apostle Paul consistently and forcefully warns against such behavior in his letters.[116]

From the secular angle, Professors Michael Norton and Elizabeth Dunn write in *Happy Money*[117] that spending on experiences and on other people will bring more lasting happiness than spending on material possessions. As one of our interviewees volunteered, "[spending on] experiences, community, and travel more than a fancy house or possessions is a decision we feel good about looking back through the rearview mirror." With regard to fancy houses and possessions, both of us (John and Greg) have admitted to one another that we had ultimate home-price targets in the one to two million dollar range before beginning this project, which represented our desire for status and a prideful display of earning power, rather than the physical need to keep a roof over our families' heads, which can be accomplished with a far lower number.

Brandon Fremont explained to us that he keeps an active list of "potential budget cuts" on his iPhone at all times. He periodically reviews this list and makes a cut, reporting that it usually doesn't

---

116 Kotter, David, "Working for the Glory of God," PhD Dissertation at Southern Baptist Theological Seminary, 2015. 88.

117 Dunn, Elizabeth and Norton, Michael, *Happy Money: The Science of Happier Spending*, Simon and Schuster, 2013.

hurt nearly as much as he expects. Such active stewardship over a spending budget is an inspiration to us, and a potential best practice with regard to identifying truly life-giving spending versus unnecessary comforts that don't add much value to our lives.

Clearly, by John Paul II's framework, high spending on material goods both violates the empirically verified principles from *Happy Money* and fails to enhance a human sense of "being." He identifies such spending as "superdevelopment," which is a mirror-image tragedy to the underdevelopment of the poor. (As Proverbs 30:8 says, "give me neither poverty nor riches.") Anyone familiar with the classic work *The Millionaire Next Door*[118] might immediately think of Dr. South, the neurosurgeon profiled in the book whose family spends the entirety of their $700,000 income, with $104,000 allocated to the mortgage and $30,000 spent annually on clothing alone. We wonder what Dr. South would have said if he had been able to listen to the Samuels family tell their story. Income, properly spent, brings human fulfillment and joy up to the point where we can fully walk out our calling in life. When taken beyond that point, consumption becomes wasteful, a misappropriation of resources and a slap in the face of the poor whom God calls us to care for. Thus, increased spending power does not necessarily equate to human flourishing; rather, high spending power enables the possibility of human flourishing, if and only if the funds are spent wisely.

UNIVERSAL AND HEALTHY DESIRES FOR FLOURISHING

So, getting back to the ultimate question: how much should be consumed, and how much should be allocated toward saving and giving? By thinking about your family budget in terms of Maslow's

---

118 Stanley, Thomas and Danko, William, *The Millionaire Next Door*, Simon and Schuster, 1996.

Hierarchy as seen in Figure 3, the tradeoffs become clear. A believer should consider his or her role as appointed by God, balancing the mandate to contribute to the Kingdom with the God-given desire to provide for current and future human needs. Even for those in poverty, the wisdom and godliness of saving and giving remains present, although such a family could spend a clear majority of their financial resources while still honoring God's word in every way. (The tithe of someone earning $50,000 may represent greater faithfulness than the one million dollar check written by someone earning three million dollars!)

For those earning upper-middle class incomes approaching six figures, saving and giving should each gain more prominence in the budget, since basic human needs have already been met. Each incremental dollar of earnings can be split between lifestyle improvements and giving or saving. Once the first cut has been given and some funds have been saved, remaining income can be used to create further opportunities of human flourishing for one's family. For those earning well into the six-figure range, a new and interesting problem arises. Should spending continue to increase without limit? Or, in order to avoid the tragedy of "superdevelopment"—excessive spending that does not increase human flourishing—should there be a ceiling on consumption?

We believe the answer is yes, and the finish line of $150,000 in Figure 3 was in fact chosen quite intentionally. We dug into a variety of sources in order to understand spending from the most scientific, rigorous perspective possible for our own future planning. It is our belief after this research that estimates of a universally desired lifestyle usually hone in on spending power in the low-six figures range. Anecdotally, this is a level of spending we have observed among our family friends and business associates which seems to more than adequately support the reasonable desires of a typical family.

It is also corroborated by additional sources. *USA Today* recently attempted to discover how much spending is required to realize the American Dream and settled at a value of around $60,000 for "the essentials" and somewhat over $100,000 to fully enjoy an American life (approximately $120,000 pre-tax).[119] Thomas Piketty, in his best-seller *Capital in the Twenty-First Century*, claims that even in feudal Europe there was a notion of a universally desired lifestyle, consisting of the ability to travel, to dress and dine well, to become educated, and to pursue the arts.[120] The nobility were the only ones lucky enough to achieve such a lifestyle, but novelists such as Jane Austen described with great detail what such a lifestyle consisted of and the budgetary outlays necessary to sustain it. This lifestyle, more or less, might reflect John Paul II's notion of fulfilling the "human vocation." According to Piketty's purchasing-power adjustments, such a lifestyle can be financed with two to three times the average income in the Western world today, or roughly $100,000 to $150,000 of after-tax spending. Rounding up for modern taxes, Piketty's values correspond to total income of approximately $120,000 to $200,000. (Amazingly, then, the top five to ten percent of families in the United States can finance lifestyles equal to or better than the Lords and Dukes of Old Europe.)

It is remarkable how these three independent sources converge, indicating that somewhere between family incomes of $120,000 and $200,000 there is an intersection between the lifestyles of Old European nobility, the modern American Dream, and perhaps even a biblical vision of healthy flourishing from a material perspective. Even the tax code seems to acknowledge this, with the largest jump in marginal income tax rates occurring at the low end of this income range, as if the government deems that once a

---

119 USA Today, "Price tag for the American dream," http://www.usatoday.com/story/money/ personalfinance /2014/07/04/american-dream/11122015/, accessed November, 2014.

120 Piketty, Thomas, *Capital in the Twenty-First Century*, Harvard University Press, 2014, 415.

family's material needs have been well-provided for, their tax-take can then increase dramatically.[121] This is not a lifestyle of endless luxury, but one which enables its beneficiaries to enjoy their lives richly, without concern for meeting material deficiencies.

If gross income of $200,000, corresponding to spending power of roughly $150,000 per year in 2016, represents a high-end estimate of what a universally desired lifestyle consists of, what can we conclude? First of all, spending should be healthily constrained within one's income in a way that allows for some saving and giving. We also propose that, once enough income has been earned to flourish and pursue the desires common to all people, spending should cease to depend on income. As one survey response put it, "I think we should set an 'income' for ourselves, and give the rest away." In economic terms, this means that there is an income above which a Christian's marginal propensity to consume should fall to zero. This is not necessarily true for all people, but for believers, whose call is to share their possessions with those in need, support the expansion of the Kingdom, and to look out for the least of these, the impetus should become clear.

Looking at these facts, we both realized it was time for us to get serious about preventing spending from ruling over our lives. We wanted to be able to bless our families with nice things, but not become consumed by consumption. Thus, following the example of some of our case studies, we both set for ourselves Spending Finish Lines. This Finish Line was established after careful consideration and prayer, and represents the devotion of excess income to other purposes—namely, saving and giving.

---

121 In 2015, the Married Filing Joint Return bracket jumps from 15 percent to 25 percent at $74,900 in taxable income, corresponding to gross income of about $125,000 according to our estimates and overall cash spending power of about $100,000. (We assume itemized deductions of $26,800, which is the average for six-figure earners, personal exemptions of $3,800 multiplied by four family members, and medical premiums and deductions of $10,000. 401k contributions would allow for even higher earnings without broaching the 25 percent line, up to $142,800).

A $100,000 budget, which we each chose as our upper-limit, is just an example arrived at by triangulating a set of diverse sources. For us, this becomes the vertical line on the Servant's Money Map, dividing "I could use some more income" from "I make plenty of income." The value for each family following suit could be higher and certainly might be lower. In fact, lower is better in terms of quickly obtaining financial freedom. It is far easier to become financially independent with a lifestyle costing less than $100,000 per year than it is to achieve it when spending many multiples of that. The lower we set our consumption behaviors, the faster we can obtain financial freedom and begin giving more aggressively to Christ's work in the world.

By setting spending patterns at 80 to 100 percent of income or higher in most of modern society, we constrain ourselves to the consumeristic treadmill of never-ending working and spending. We will be a slave to something when it comes to money. Should we be a slave to spending? Those with lower incomes may have to be, but for higher-income individuals, choosing to be a slave to spending seems illogical when compared with people like the Samuels, who have a vision of their money that is far grander in scope. Although our finish lines are $100,000 per year in spending, we have ambitions to see whether we can live more modestly and experience abundant life that is not reliant upon high levels of cash flow. If we find that we can live on $70,000, we aren't going to blow an extra $30,000 in December just to make it to the limit!

We recognize, of course, that aging parents, children with special needs, or extended family in need of support could all drive spending much higher (although it could be argued that some of these cases could be considered giving rather than spending—the distinction becomes mere semantics at some point). There is nothing magical about the precise numbers we've chosen for our own upper limits, but the implication of rough agreement around them from multiple sources is that a Christian would need a quite good reason to spend significantly more than this—the vast majority of society seems to get along quite nicely within this range, and such a lifestyle was considered aristocratic for most of human history. Once a limit is set, spending will no longer bear any relationship to income. Even if my income suddenly increased by one million dollars next year, I commit to saying, "Wow, what a blessing! Our spending needs are already met, so we will prayerfully allocate these newfound funds to giving and to saving." This concept is demonstrated graphically below. Funds available to give or save can increase to infinity, but personal consumption is capped by a carefully considered limit.

Table 7: Spending Finish Line Illustration

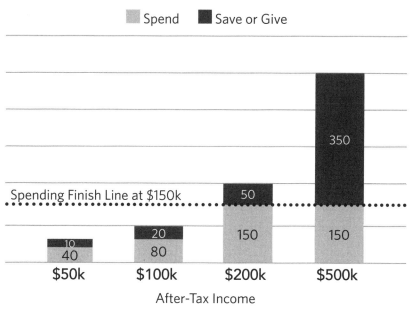

While this idea seems radical on its surface, there is ample precedent in the cloud of witnesses for such a choice.

- Rich Mullins, the immensely successful Christian musician of the 1990s, told his accountant to give him the average American income and to give the excess away.[122] Knowing how money had begun to corrupt him early in his career, he turned a blind eye toward his actual income, never knowing how much money his music actually earned.

- Alan Barnhart, a modern Christian business leader, takes a fixed salary of roughly $140,000 to support himself, his wife, and his six children. He is quick to point out this is "not sacrificial" since it is 3.5 times the poverty line.[123, 124] Meanwhile, he has given over $100 million of excess income to Christian charities around the world, involving his children in the philanthropic process along the way. His lifestyle is fixed, while his generosity grows with his earning power.

- Similarly, Will Pope, our oil and gas CEO from Oklahoma, draws a salary a bit over $200,000 per year and gives all of his upside away to Christian development work in the third world.

- RG LeTourneau[125] and Rick Warren[126] have both helped to popularize the "reverse tithe"—giving 90 percent of their incomes away for the Gospel.

---

122 Beeman, Patrick, "Rich Mullins, Asymptotic Catholic," http://www.firstthings.com/web-exclusives/2013/03/rich-mullins-asymptotic-catholic, accessed November, 2014.

123 Generous Testimony: Alan Barnhart, YouTube, uploaded May 10, 2012. https://www.youtube.com/watch?v=m0__rBqEr3Y, accessed October 2014.

124 Authors' conversation with an associate of Mr. Barnhart indicates that $140,000 is the most recent salary figure as of 2014, and that expenses supported by this salary include at least some spending on college tuition for children.

125 Giants for God, "RG LeTourneau, Earthmoving Innovator," http://www.giantsforgod.com/rg-letourneau/, accessed November, 2014.

126 Warren, Rick, Big Think, "What is a reverse tithe?" http://bigthink.com/videos/what-is-a-reverse-tithe, accessed November, 2014.

These are a few examples among many of Christians who have submitted their financial success to the Lord in beautiful ways and have put spending in its proper place, subservient to our call to be Servants of Christ with our money. Our hope is that this framework can help many others join their ranks.

PARTING THOUGHT—*HOW DO WE SPEND?*

One final note on spending—when we take on the mindset of a Servant, our spending may change in character. One family that spent just $50,000 on themselves every year ended up spending an extra $30,000 on rehabilitating and supporting a child they welcomed into their home for a year. Did they "spend" $50,000 or $80,000 that year? We don't know how to handle the accounting, but we do know that we want to emulate their Servant hearts.

For a Closer Look . . .

Pastor Jeff Manion led the growth of Ada Bible Church in western Michigan from just 25 members to over 8,000 today. He has written a book on contentment called *Satisfied.* Listen to him share on this topic in this inspiring 15-minute clip, "Here & Now," at GodandMoney. net/resources.

We've heard of vision trips to Africa replacing European getaways. Or perhaps you begin regularly buying lunch for people and hosting groups in your home, intentionally sharing the love of Christ with others. You hire the out-of-work friend at church to paint your house, knowing that you could have done it yourself, but preferring to give him the dignity of work. One couple we know acquired a few acres of land, eagerly hosting youth groups and visiting missionaries at their impromptu retreat center. Our point is, it will be a life beautifully lived if you can begin to blur the lines between Spending and Serving.

If you have trouble deciding what counts as giving and what counts as spending . . . you're probably doing it right. If you're a very high-income believer, it would be far better to spend $150,000 per year in a life that is invitational to others, generous and hospitable, than to spend $80,000 per year by becoming insular, isolated, and miserly, clipping coupons, tipping stingily, and cutting yourself off from others. There is a danger in this, because it would be quite easy to spend a lot of money, with the subtle self-justification of "at least I'm generous in spirit." To get this right requires a *serious shift* in mindset to become oriented toward others. A generous lifestyle should not preclude cutting large checks to effective ministries, but we also believe that high-income families should leave some margin for spending that builds community, honors God, and blesses those in their sphere of influence. There is great joy in living this way!

CHAPTER SEVEN

Saving—Investing in the Future

"And do not seek what you are to eat and what you are to drink, nor be worried. . . . Instead, seek his kingdom, and these things will be added to you."
—Jesus, Luke 12:29-31

"Do not toil to acquire wealth;
be discerning enough to desist."
—Proverbs 23:4

After spending is taken care of, how should excess income be distributed between giving and saving? Should we even save at all? The Christian life contains a tension between the sovereignty of God and the responsibility of man. We plan the future by revealed wisdom—and we pray for specific revelation. We visit doctors and take medicine—and we ask for healing, trusting God for health. We give out of trust—and we save out of godly responsibility. As New Testament followers of Jesus, we have one foot in the eternal future, but the other is still firmly planted in earthly realities. His Kingdom is here, but it is also not yet. We believe saving has a valid place in the life of a Christian. However, it is not to be an assumed place, nor is it to be an exalted place. Our savings goals have to be subjugated to our desire to glorify God, and put through the test of whether they have become an idol in our hearts. And all savings, at all times, should be held openly before the Lord for His guidance and, perhaps, His instructions to give them away (Luke 18:22).

We believe that as Servants, our call is to carefully weigh the savings vs. giving decision according to the priority of the needs around us. Anything we save ought to be attached to a tangible goal or need. Highly pressing personal needs might take priority in the early stages of wealth accumulation, while those with more resources can afford to focus their incremental attention on giving. We must weigh the worthiness of different wealth objectives, knowing that the alternative for our money is to give it away for the benefit of the Church or the poor. The following sections explore this trade-off for the most commonly shared reasons to accumulate wealth: freedom from consumer debt, home ownership, educating children, and retirement in old age. We categorize these needs as "The Basics," representing nearly universal human needs and desires. "Luxuries" in our framework represent anything beyond this, including financial independence, business equity, etc. We will explore how to approach each of these wealth objectives as a servant of Christ.

For each category, we'll present a reasonable personal finance guideline, our finish line, and our personal status, followed by some analysis. Our analysis stands on our study of Scripture, best practices in Christian personal finance today, and our original research and case studies. We'll move quickly. Clearly, a whole book or set of books could be written on this chapter alone, but we want to present our biblically informed thinking with brevity. There are many sources of more detailed personal finance recommendations, such as the Compass Map, Ron Blue's teaching on Biblical Financial Principles, Dave Ramsey's Seven Baby Steps, and the Money Mindset research conducted by Thrivent Financial. As always, we want to emphasize that every case is different, and the purpose of the specific monetary values that follow is to be illustrative, not prescriptive. Nonetheless, we will employ real dollar figures, because we believe they are more concrete and useful than simply discussing abstract ideas.[127]

The Basics

"Aspire to live quietly, and to mind your own affairs, and to work with your hands, as we instructed you, so that you may walk properly before outsiders and be dependent on no one."
—The apostle Paul, 1 Thessalonians 4:11-12

Freedom from Consumer Debt (Own Cars Outright and Have an Emergency Fund)

- **Personal Finance Guideline:** Pay off the debt. Pay cash for cars. Keep three to six month's expenses in an emergency fund.

- **Our Finish Lines:** Debt-freedom, two cars worth no more than $30,000 each, and a $40,000 emergency fund.

- **Our Status:** The Cortines family graduated with $50,000 in student loans on a seven-year payoff plan. We have two cars worth a combined $18,000. We're saving out of cash flow for newer cars and to build up our emergency fund, which stands at $10,000 currently. The Baumer family graduated

---

127 All figures are in 2016 dollars, and should be inflation adjusted into the future.

with $180,000 in student loans on a four-year payoff plan. Their two cars are also worth a total of $18,000 and their emergency fund is now mostly funded, at $35,000.

Consumer debt, defined here as all non-mortgage debt held by a household, generally represents negative net worth. This includes car loans, student loans, credit-card debt, and payday loans.[128] When in consumer debt, both Savers and Servants will probably choose to allocate a relatively large fraction of income toward debt repayment, rather than spending or giving.

Student loans are quickly becoming the most pervasive, almost ubiquitous, consumer debt. We each intend to pay off our graduate student loans relatively quickly, which could at times be a constraint to short-term giving. We disagree, however, with those personal finance gurus who suggest debt repayment should totally subordinate giving. Regular giving is important for maintaining personal well-being and obedience to God's Word. Even though we each carry substantial student loans, it seems ludicrous to think that we would stop giving completely in order to pay them off more quickly.

For some who have lived their lives in a state of "superdevelopment," to use John Paul II's term, responsible choices in this area of wealth may involve choosing a more modest car than is affordable for their income level. One individual we know cancelled his order for a $185,000 Audi R8 after reading Randy Alcorn's *The Treasure Principle*, realizing that an investment in eternity would be a more exciting use of the money. Similarly, Will Pope's accountability group challenged his ownership of a Mercedes. He began to realize the car was all about ego for him personally, and swapped it for a

---

128   There are certain advanced cases in which a person might choose to obtain consumer debt, despite having enough money to pay it off (for example, taking a car loan at a one-percent interest rate, and then investing the money in the stock market, hoping to earn more than one-percent returns). This analysis ignores such cases and assumes that the reason for consumer debt is simply that funds are not available to pay it off.

non-luxury SUV. We are absolutely not suggesting that owning a luxury car is a fundamental problem, but we do suggest that it should not be an automatic choice for those with the money to buy one. For Will, it was a threat to the health of his own heart and spiritual walk, and he humbly recognized this—what an honest and Christ-centered way to live!

Driving a very old car has turned out to have unexpected spiritual benefits. As minor breakdowns have occurred in my 2006 Honda Odyssey, I've noticed God working on my heart. Sitting in an auto shop, having lost three hours and $400 due to a minor breakdown, is frustrating. But then I think—this is how a huge fraction of the world lives their lives! I am so spoiled, frankly, that experiences such as this are abnormal in my life. Not to mention the blessing it is that I have easy access to $400 to cover the repairs. Driving an old, beat-up car is a situation that God has used to heighten my sense of compassion and solidarity with those who have less than I do. I look forward to the day when my family might pay cash for a brand new minivan, but for now, I'm enjoying the lessons God is teaching me with a very old one.

Finally, we believe that maintaining an emergency fund of three to six months' worth of expenses makes sense for our families. This is the standard recommendation in personal finance for all families. This fits in line with Paul's exhortations to believers that they should care for their families, work with their hands, and avoid becoming a burden to others. Such a fund protects against unexpected job loss, the need for a new roof, health calamities, and a million other possibilities.

Reflection Point:

- How much are our cars worth?

- How much is in our emergency fund?

- Do we have consumer debts?

- Should we set a finish line for these items, and if so, how much should it be?

Home Ownership

- **Personal Finance Guideline:** Payments less than 28 percent of income. Home value no more than three to four times your income.

- **Our Finish Lines:** In normal geographies, look for no more than 3,000 square feet with five bedrooms, which typically costs less than $500,000 unless local real estate conditions are exceptional. Will not spend more than what we can qualify for on a 15-year mortgage, counting only 80 percent of our income.

- **Our Status:** In 2015, the Cortines family bought a $295,000 home with 2,500 square feet, in a modestly priced suburban area, with a 30-year loan they plan to pay off in 10 to 20 years. The Baumer family is home shopping and will likely spend over $500,000 for a modest, older home due to a hot real estate market in Nashville near Greg's work location. They plan on a 30-year payoff plan in order to give more along the way.

Housing is a tricky subject. Every local market is different, and there are a multitude of factors that influence the decision to purchase a home. As Brandon Fremont put it, "Home buying is a multivariable optimization problem. I'd like a house in a neighborhood with high diversity, a low crime rate, reasonable pricing, a wonderful school district, and lots of open space. Oh, and I'd like for it to be within a 10-minute drive from my office, ideally on the same side of town as my church." Obviously, such a home does not exist! Therefore, sacrifices will have to be made on one or more dimensions when choosing a home.

It is this complexity that gave us pause when we considered how much we could generalize. The empty nesters in a $600,000, 6,000 square foot McMansion in a suburb of Texas may be making a much more wasteful decision than the family in a $1.5 million modest apartment in a very expensive city. So, drawing bright lines with respect to price alone would be an exercise in futility. The decision must be managed with an eye for the needs of the family seeking a home, with the heart of a Servant rather than a Spender or Saver. Will we be comfortable discussing our choice of home with Jesus, when we see him face to face?

Table 8: Typical cost for a 2,000–3,000 square foot, 4-bedroom home within commuting distance to downtown

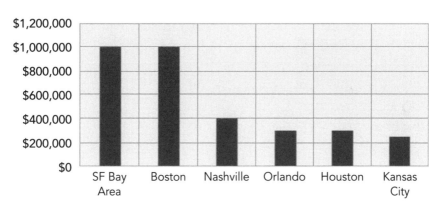

Most people we've met who live in large, luxury homes have a good reason for it. They love to host. They got a really good deal. They've made a lot of money on the appreciation. People occasionally spend a few nights with them. It is not anyone's place to cast judgment on any particular decision made by someone else in a gray area such as this, but we have noticed that no one says, "I love the way owning this house makes me feel about myself, and I derive self-worth from knowing that I live in the most exclusive neighborhood in town."

Our case studies couldn't be further from such a mindset. Denise and her husband live in a 2,000 square foot home they purchased decades ago. Edward and Katherine Heath, whose case study will appear in the next chapter, own a $450,000 home, despite the ability to easily purchase a home in the low one millions. Last year they prayerfully considered upgrading neighborhoods, but concluded that doing so would be out of prideful desires for status, rather than a legitimate need. They have seen many friends upgrade neighborhoods and have observed how doing so tends to turn Toyotas into Lexuses, and how family trips to the beach become overseas luxury vacations. When surrounded by Spenders, it is hard to resist the urge to join in and become one yourself.

Choosing a home that is, first of all, affordable, and second of all, sufficient without being excessive, is the guiding principle we have chosen to adopt after conducting our research and speaking with many generous Christians whom we admire. The average new home built in America was 1,650 square feet in the 1970s, but is over 2,500 square feet today.[129] Median square footage has actually increased 10 percent from 2008 to 2013. We continue to build larger and larger homes even after the housing crash! We are truly in an era of extremes in our pursuit of ever more luxurious living spaces; there may be wisdom in eschewing the big mortgage by choosing a more modest home which can be paid off quickly.

Servants should avoid referencing "home affordability calculators" online without making careful modifications to them. Such

---

129   Daily Finance, "Does your home live up to the American average?" http://www.dailyfinance.com/on/average-us-home-size-features/#!fullscreen&slide=2712446, accessed March, 2015.

calculators don't consider the fact that you are a giver. Remember, six out of seven families don't give at all—they, not you, are for whom the calculators are designed! Our chosen method is to see what we can afford based on 80 percent of our income on a 15-year loan, and this gives us limits barely *half* what the calculators initially told us we could afford, and puts us in a much more flexible position to live as Servants.

How quickly should a home be paid off? We know people who have paid off their house as fast as possible, and others who stick to a 30-year schedule in order to give more away today. One friend who paid his house off reflected to us, "You know, life doesn't feel that different. People make mortgage payoff this huge deal, and yes, it's nice to be free of it. But taxes and insurance are still there, maintenance and utilities don't go away, and my lifestyle hasn't changed at all. There's just some more cash at the end of each month . . . and so what? I wish I had known it wasn't such a big deal after all to finally pay it off." We understand the desire to eliminate the mortgage, but we've each decided to take at least 10 years to pay our homes off, even though we might be able to do it sooner. We'd rather give, or save for other goals, than obsess over this one. If we build enough equity such that we're headed toward a 10-year payoff, we'll simply stop putting money on the mortgage and focus on other priorities.

The idea of raising our families in reasonably "normal" surroundings, as opposed to the most elite setting we can afford, also offers a chance to help our children grow up more grounded and in-touch. In fact, for this reason we (the Cortines family) purchased a home which is among the nicest in our neighborhood. Conventional wisdom says to buy the cheapest house in a neighborhood, but we felt that doing so would put us among neighbors who would outspend our lifestyles, presenting a danger to our hearts. Rather, being among the most expensive homes in our neighborhood allows our more frugal spending tendencies to feel "normal" relative to that of our neighbors.

Finally, no matter what home we buy, we should always remember that it is really God's home, not ours. Keeping in mind our role as stewards of His possessions will help us have perspective on how we should use what is often the most valuable thing entrusted to us—our home.

Reflection Point:

■ What's the value of our house, or homes?

■ What's our payoff plan?

■ Is there a finish line in sight for how much capital we want to tie up in a home?

■ How can we put our house to work for the Kingdom?

RETIREMENT

■ **Personal Finance Guideline:** Save at least 15 percent of your income. If you can, max out all available accounts. If you finish early, nice job.

■ **Our Finish Lines:** Save no more than is necessary to generate our spending finish line in perpetuity, from age 67 forward.[130] If we start getting ahead of pace, consider cutting back savings.

■ **Our Status:** The Cortines family has about $150,000 saved and now saves $12,000 to $17,000 per year. The Baumer family has about $100,000 saved and is currently saving

---

130 Our spreadsheet tool, or your financial advisor, can help calculate this if you aren't comfortable with the calculations and assumptions involved.

$15,000 to $17,000 per year. Neither family has plans to save more aggressively in the foreseeable future.[131]

Learning what a Servant mindset around retirement looks like has been the biggest stumbling block for me (John) in our entire journey in researching this book. For me, early retirement has always been a highly prized objective—the shining promise of financial freedom, out in the distance like a tempting oasis. My multi-tab, probabilistic spreadsheets used to tell me I could get there in my mid-forties if I saved aggressively enough in my Chevron career.

Denise Whitfield, still happily working at 61 as a financial advisor, played a part in shattering my imperfect perspective. She mused that "all of my clients want to retire at 50, but for what? Retirement is an artificial construct. [Retiring at 50] moves the fulcrum too far to the left, such that no room is left for anything but aggressive savings! People act as if there is some template we have to all follow, whereby we must stop working as soon as we can because that's what everyone says to do. Rather, let's ask the Lord what He would have us do for each year of our life." For a Saver like me, this sounded crazy, but I slowly began to realize that Denise was demonstrating the very core of the Servant mentality around wealth.

Similarly, Brandon Fremont views retirement savings as something to gradually work toward in support of financial security in old age, when he is no longer capable of working. He wants to have three million dollars for retirement when he is old enough to no longer be able to work. But he's taking a slow path of accumulation to get there, with no plans to stop working, despite his enormous

---

131 Our figures include company matching contributions. Naturally, we will always take advantage of any "free money" available for matching, even if it means we need to divest from some other accounts to avoid over-accumulation.

earning power. If I were in his shoes, I might save for one or two years and then call it quits! But he faithfully keeps working, giving, and sharing from his tremendous resources. Why allocate a huge portion of disposable income toward retirement today, when he has decades to keep saving for it?

Financial expert Mitch Anderson points out that retirement, as an idea, originated in the industrial revolution when people traded physical labor for money from a company. Today, however, we trade our brain power for money. Does our brain stop working at 50, or 62, or 67? Mitch paints a picture for us: "It's day 42 of your retirement, the alarm goes off, and you realize that you have no reason or purpose for getting out of bed. What do you do now?"[132] There are many cases where we may desire a transition out of high-earning fields to do more missional work, but laboring hard with purpose is something we should plan to do as Servants for as long as the Lord gives us life and a functioning mind.

I was really proud of the fact that I was socking away over $35,000 per year in retirement savings as a 23-year-old, maxing out every account type I could find. Such aggressive savings were needed to support my plan to potentially retire early, kick back, and fade into the sunset. I now plan to continue using my abilities productively until I am no longer able to—to age 70, God willing. If I run the numbers now, it becomes clear that I need to put away far less each year to have enough at the end of my life—the fulcrum is now in the right place. I now simply save enough to get my full 401k match, and also contribute to my wife Megan's Roth IRA. (She works hard as a stay-at-home mother, and deserves to accumulate retirement funds just as much as I do.)

To conclude, we have come to believe that saving for retirement is wise in the right context, but overly aggressive accumulation

---

132 Talk given to Kingdom Advisors regional conference in New York, New York. September 15, 2015.

prioritizes personal comfort above our mandate to share the Gospel and the love of Christ with the world. We have decided that if we start getting ahead of pace on saving for an old-age retirement, we'll scale back, allowing us to give more or save in other areas in the present.

Reflection Point:

- Are we on track, ahead of pace, or behind pace?

- How long should we work in our current capacities, with a Servant mentality?

COLLEGE FOR CHILDREN

- **Personal Finance Guideline:** Open 529 accounts and save according to expected future expenses.

- **Our Finish Lines:** Prayerfully save an amount for each child that covers the majority, but not the full totality, of their overall anticipated college expenses.

- **Our Status:** We have each opened 529 accounts, with plans to save up a modest five-figure sum for each child before they graduate from high school. The specifics will evolve depending on college price inflation, potential for each child to earn scholarships, financial aid possibilities, etc., and cannot be predicted with precision at this time.

Most parents, if financially able, would like to provide for their children's education. In the modern age, a college degree has almost become a prerequisite for entry into the middle to upper-middle class. Scripture clearly teaches that we should provide for our own families, and we believe this expense represents something that any able parent should consider paying, assuming that a child has demonstrated the maturity and godliness to warrant such an investment. The difference between finishing an undergraduate degree with a few dollars in the bank, versus finishing with $60,000 in loans, is enormous in the life of a twenty-something. As we are able, we hope to put our own children in the former situation, if they work diligently to use the gifts God has given them and follow His calling for their lives.

This goal probably ranks in a similar place with retirement savings for a responsible wealth steward. It is natural and proper to desire the best for one's children, as a reflection of how our heavenly Father desires the best for us. However, accumulating wealth for children aggressively, at the expense of giving opportunities, deprives children of a chance to see their family's money at work in the Christian community, and could foster an insular attitude within the family that is at odds with the emphasis on shared, communal life presented to us in Scripture.

One of us recently visited a wealthy Christian family whose daughter had a map, with pictures, of the fifty children in third-world nations that her family actively sponsors. She helps write letters to them and prays for their well-being. Such an involvement in family generosity is a wonderful thing for a young child, perhaps ranking every bit as important as future tuition.

Reflection Point:.

- What's the most likely situation with regard to our children's higher education?

- How are we preparing? Are we going too far, or not far enough?

REFLECTION ON THE BASICS

For all of The Basics, my desire had always been to save up as quickly as possible, so that I could feel secure. I realize now, however, that God is my provider—not my own superior planning abilities. Saying that "God is my provider" does not absolve me from my obligations to save wisely, plan ahead, and make good choices. However, it does mean that I might choose to give rather than save, save, and save until I have all of my desires met before giving beyond my tithe to God's work. My prayer in life seems to have always been, "God, if you allow me to pay off my house by age 35, and also to save enough for all my kids to have fully funded college educations, and get my retirement savings finished, (oh, and did I mentioned that I want a red C-class Mercedes, too?) then I will start giving 15 percent or more instead of 10 percent." Such an attitude sounds a bit like Jacob's when he said, effectively, "If the Lord will do X, Y, and Z for me, then He will be my God" (See Genesis 28:20).

Instead of this old, scarcity-driven mindset, I'm trying to actively walk into a mindset of abundance that recognizes God's sovereignty over my affairs even when I don't have everything I could ever want paid for already. This has been a real challenge for me in taking a nonprofit role rather than a high-paying expatriate assignment, but God has been faithful to teach me contentment in a new circumstance. With a spirit of abundance, and the mindset of a Servant, I hope to make generous gifts to Christ's kingdom even now, as I trust in Him for all future provision.

Brandon Fremont illustrates these principles beautifully in his own life. He intentionally chooses to avoid obtaining financial independence, despite earning millions each year. In fact, he uses insurance strategically, as a way to reduce his need for wealth accumulation. "Why would you set aside money beyond [The Basics]? Only for fear of disability, death, and the choice to stop working. I buy disability insurance and life insurance to cover [the possibility of disability or death]. And work is a privilege—the concept of a retirement to just relax is not in Scripture, and it doesn't make sense. I spend $2,500 per year to cover my family in case I become disabled or die, and otherwise I plan to keep working." He sees no need to accumulate further savings—a choice that enables him to give in magnificent ways within his church community here and now.

Reflection Point: For most American families, The Basics cost under one million dollars. John and Greg set their finish line at this value for *all* of the Basics.

- Do we want to set a finish line?

- Given our family situation and local cost of living, what would this look like?

LUXURIES

> *"What the rich should do with the superfluous—with that which goes beyond the necessities and is therefore a burden—is to distribute it to those in need."*
> —Clement of Alexandria

FINANCIAL INDEPENDENCE

- **Personal Finance Guideline:** Keep saving! Maybe one day you can stop working!

- **Our Finish Lines:** Only accumulate more than The Basics if there's a good reason. Never, under any circumstances, accumulate more than 33 times our Spending Finish Line in a Financial Independence fund. (Limit: $3.3 million.[133])

- **Our Status:** Neither of us has yet finished saving for The Basics, so we're not on this step yet.

---

133   This figure is a capitalized version of our spending finish line. A portfolio worth 33 times one's spending finish line can roughly generate the finish line in investment earnings every year.

Financial Independence could be alternatively defined as early retirement, or at least the accumulation of enough funds such that one could retire early if he or she wanted to. It represents a level of wealth which can finance a lifestyle in perpetuity, meaning the owner never needs to work again.

While the goals represented by The Basics are fairly standard, the reasons behind seeking financial independence would be highly unique to each individual. It is critical to ask what is the purpose of this further accumulation of wealth? Some dream of having the freedom to attend graduate school, enter ministry, pursue the arts, or teach. Others, planning to keep their jobs, perhaps envision a sense of security and ease that will come with knowing that a paycheck is truly not needed.

Given the condemnation of the Rich Fool, we believe that pursuing Financial Independence should be done very carefully, if at all. A simple desire for security may not be reason enough, although this is something each believer must wrestle with individually. Once all The Basics have been realized, a steward must take care to not overemphasize continued accumulation of resources. Cyprian, an early Church father, railed passionately against the behavior of those who sought to save up continually more money simply for the sake of personal security.[134]

We have met families who eschew financial independence, as well as those who have carefully, prayerfully embraced it, and we respect either choice when it is made with intentionality. Will Pope, for example, maintains liquid investments worth millions of dollars—his "Personal Wealth Finish Line" fund. Having this fund securely in place allows him and his family to focus on viewing their business as a tool for God's glory, fully released from

---

134   Gonzalez, Justo. *Faith and Wealth: A History of Early Christian Ideas on the Origin, Significance, and Use of Money,* Wipf and Stock, 1990, 127.

their grasp. If the business imploded tomorrow, they would be OK, and this allows them to give generously without hesitation from ongoing profits, with no savings whatsoever. They also make sure they do not become attached even to their fund. Will says, "There are no guarantees and the market could crash. I'm in God's hands and don't worry about it. We can move back to Costa Rica and live in a 700 square foot apartment [if we needed to]." Their Personal Wealth Finish Line is a fixed quantity, too. When the value of the fund recently increased due to market appreciation, they sold off the profits and gave them away, keeping the value of the fund constant.

Within our framework, we view The Basics as the "floor" for how much wealth we intend to accumulate, and financial independence as the "ceiling." Whether we will someday land at our floor or our ceiling will be a judgment call made under the accountability of our brothers and sisters in Christ. Once decided upon, this value will represent the horizontal line in the Servant's Money Map—delineating how much wealth is "enough" for us. For now, we'll each begin the slow journey toward paying for all of The Basics, knowing that our giving will dramatically increase once we make it there.

Reflection Point:

- Do either of us have a Kingdom purpose that would lead us to pursue Financial Independence?

- What would the finish line amount be?

ADDING IT ALL UP

Summing up The Basics for both the Baumer and Cortines families represents a net worth around one million dollars in 2016 dollars. This is based on our current plans, which include a longer-term savings path for retirement, homes under half a million dollars, modest college savings, and non-luxury cars. (Our prior plans in life required as much as three million dollars for The Basics, including one to two million dollar homes and early retirements. It's noteworthy how lifestyle choices can bring financial constraint or freedom.) Financial independence requires approximately an additional three million dollars for either of our families, so we view this value as the absolute upper limit on wealth accumulation in our lives.

So long as we are north of one million dollars but south of four million dollars,[135] active and intentional stewardship will be required to guide the giving away or accumulation of funds. Above four million dollars, we will "chop off" the top of our net worth, following Will Pope's example. Below one million dollars, we will strive to gain wealth as we make provision for our families. In between the two values, we will prayerfully consider our situation and make active decisions about whether or not to increase our personal wealth. If we are about to quit our job to pursue low-income ministry, we may trend toward the higher value; if we feel like we are going to keep working in high-paying jobs for many years to come, we'll steer closer to the lower number. This decision framework is summarized by the graphic below.

Figure 4: Personal Wealth Finish Line Framework

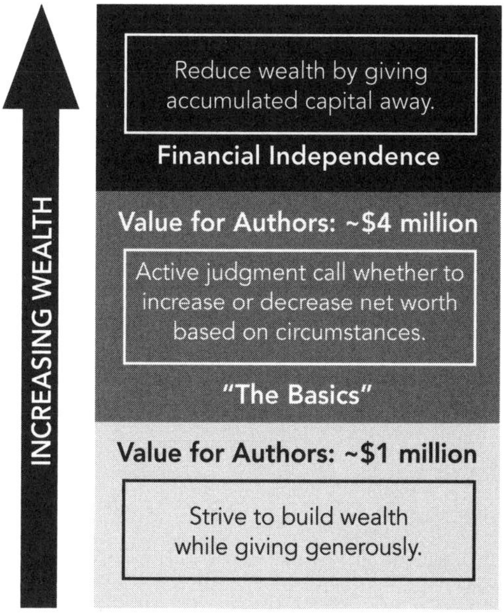

INCREASING WEALTH

Reduce wealth by giving accumulated capital away.

Financial Independence

Value for Authors: ~$4 million

Active judgment call whether to increase or decrease net worth based on circumstances.

"The Basics"

Value for Authors: ~$1 million

Strive to build wealth while giving generously.

---

135   On an inflation-adjusted basis.

INHERITANCE

- **Personal Finance Guideline:** Maximize value through careful estate planning. Complain about the inheritance tax and try to avoid it.

- **Our Finish Lines:** Pay for college, and provide a modest (probably $100,000 or less) amount of help beyond that, relatively early in our children's adult lives. No windfall upon our death. Involve our kids in our generosity as they mature, providing a rich spiritual heritage of giving.

- **Our Status:** We are saving for college, and will provide any further help from future cash flow or savings.

It is worth including a brief note on inheritance. Before beginning this project, both of us planned to amass the largest fortunes we could (tithing along the way) and then pass them along to our respective children. John had even begun reading books on how to preserve family fortunes across multiple generations! At this point, however, we recognize a higher calling on our wealth than giving it to our children—service to God's kingdom has to take priority. Our case studies have similar views.

We were particularly inspired by Brandon Fremont's plans. He wants to put each of his children through college, assuming that they demonstrate the aptitude and character to warrant such an investment. If they live their lives with godliness and wisdom, he then plans to help them with a down payment for their first home. And that's all. He plans to clearly communicate to each of them that this money they receive early on will be the entirety of any inheritance he leaves them. All-in, this plan will involve passing a few hundred thousand dollars to each child after age 18, including the cost of college, assuming that each is deserving. (Giving to a child living an ungodly lifestyle would represent a poor stewardship decision.)

The child benefits from receiving the wealth transfer early on, when it is more needed, and the clarity of the process is a huge benefit. From that point forward, the parents have essentially fulfilled their obligations to their children—raising them up in a Christian home, giving them good educational opportunities, and helping them become established as mature adults in society. From that point forward, the responsibility for further growth and development for each child will be their own.

A prominent financial advisor was once asked if he knew of a wealthy family that had passed its wealth down to the fourth generation with unqualified success in terms of the character and maturity of the generations involved. Despite nearly fifty years of advising prominent Christian families and leading a network of Christian financial advisors, he knew of *none*. Remember Principle Three: Wealth is like dynamite . . . and by the time it passes down a few times, someone is bound to be harmed.

One individual I met, who has earned tens of millions in his own lifetime, told me that his father let him know at age 19 that he wouldn't get a penny. It was all going to the church. He was angered and surprised at the time, but now reflects, "If he had given me a million dollars, would I have had the same drive and ambition in my own career? I can't say . . . but it sure could have changed me." He gives generously from his own earnings, and plans to give no more than a modest inheritance to his own children.

As a caveat, we'd like to point out that the inheritance of concentrated business equity, land, or other illiquid assets present a more nuanced and complicated situation than simple, liquid wealth. Given the right scenario, passing a family business or other illiquid assets to heirs could be a logical choice, but great care must be taken. Will Pope, for example, recently made the decision that his company will pass along to his children, all of whom have demonstrated *decades* of godly character and competence. They are all mature adults, and after having years of open conversations with them about this topic, he is confident they will steward the business with a Servant's heart, just as he has. He made this decision only a couple of years ago, however. He wanted to be absolutely confident that this plan would maximize the ultimate value received by God's kingdom, and thus did not always assume he would give the business to his children.

FURTHER WEALTH, BUSINESS EQUITY, ETC.

"Just a little bit more."
—John Rockefeller, when asked "How much is enough?"

- **Personal Finance Guideline:** Keep building your wealth—grow your empire.

- **Our Finish Lines:** No plans to accumulate any extra equity for the long term. If we handle some in the short-to-medium term, we will steward it wisely as belonging to God.

- **Our Status:** We each have royalties on this book, and earnings from speaking engagements. We give these away—the money goes directly to our accounts at the National Christian Foundation, and we direct it from there to various ministries. Greg has equity in his company worth a six-figure sum. He will strive to maximize its value in the short-to-medium term based on the opportunities he sees. Upon liquidation he will give and save from the proceeds according to our framework.

Once wealth has been accumulated such that The Basics are taken care of and perhaps financial independence has been attained, a strong justification is needed for any further wealth accumulation. For ourselves, we have ruled out the possibility of accumulating multiple vacation homes, ever owning a private plane, etc., because we cannot see a compelling Kingdom purpose to these things in our lives.

At this point care should also be taken to avoid an attitude of, "I'm different from most people, and my wealth-building is really helping God's Kingdom in a differentiated way." There are many among the wealthy who potentially fall into a sin of hubris; a belief that they are somehow doing God a favor by holding onto wealth and lending Him their majestic investing prowess, with the plan to give it all away upon death. We propose that it is generally better to put the money in the hands of God early on, through wise and well-planned giving, trusting in Him to multiply the investment in the spiritual realm, rather than trusting human hands to multiply the investment in the financial realm. Who are we to say that the returns earned financially would not be exceeded by the "philanthropic return" the money would have earned if it were given away early on? Even if you can legitimately generate "alpha," why not trust the One who can call Himself "the Alpha and the Omega" with the funds rather than yourself? As Denise Whitfield says, "It takes no faith whatsoever to give to Kingdom causes in your will. You don't need it when you're dead." It is easy to imagine oneself as a noble person of wealth, but it is hard to give sacrificially and reduce one's earthly possessions. We believe God will be most pleased by those who do the latter.

In fact, the literature shows that social returns on money given to some effective organizations can range from 15 to 20 percent.[136, 137] Real financial returns to an astute retail investor with a balanced index portfolio are likely to be in the realm of five percent or even less going forward.[138] Attempting to beat index returns as

---

136   For an example of the literature on Social ROI see "Returns to Investment in Education," http://isites.harvard.edu/fs/docs/icb.topic1222150.files/Session%207/PsacharopoulosGlobalUpdate.pdf

137   Jansen, Paul and Katz, David, "For Nonprofits, Time is Money," *McKinsey Quarterly*, 2002.

138   Bernstein, William, *Rational Expectations: Asset Allocation for Investing Adults*, 2014.

a retail investor is a path fraught with difficulty and danger of underperformance. According to the leading finance textbook used by Harvard Business School, efforts to beat the market by active trading or purchasing the hottest new active mutual fund are likely to result in diminished returns to a retail investor.[139] Finally, seeking excess returns through investing in alternative asset classes such as private equity funds or hedge funds, while appearing lucrative to outsiders, appears to be an inferior strategy for retail investors or endowments that are not in control of multi-billion dollar asset bases.[140]

Thus, it appears the vast majority of us are stuck with five percent future (real) returns in our financial investments, but can potentially earn 15 to 20 percent "social returns" in our giving. Additionally, giving results in an eternal prize, whereas saving poses a risk to our souls. The incentives are clear! Our desire is to live lives spoken of by Christ in Mark 4:8 about the seed on good soil, which returns 30, 60, or 100 times what was sown. Our best guess on how to get there is to give lots away, as early as we responsibly can.

Given the reasoning above, is there any reason for accumulating further riches at this stage? We do believe there are certain cases in which further wealth accumulation can be productive and useful for Christ's Kingdom. In an entrepreneurial context, the accumulation of wealth is potentially a gateway to larger and larger endeavors. Often, entrepreneurs do not consume much at all of what their labor produces, rather, they minimize their lifestyle "burn rate" and reinvest the vast majority of their wealth in

---

139 Berk, Jonathan and DeMarzo, Peter, *Corporate Finance*, Pearson, 2014, 451-452. The authors report that "typical studies find that the returns to investors of the average US equity fund has a negative alpha." and "on average actively managed mutual funds don't appear to provide superior returns for their investors compared to investing in passive index funds."

140 David Wallick, Brian Wimmer, and James Balsamo, "Assessing Endowment Performance: The Enduring Role of Low-Cost Investing," Vanguard, 2014. This study reports that "the average small or medium endowment [<$1 bn in assets] may have been better served by a portfolio of low-cost, transparent, diversified mutual funds invested in traditional stocks and bonds."

successive new businesses. The critical test in such cases is whether the illiquid business wealth is viewed as "mine" or as "God's." Such a choice should be made quite carefully and prayerfully, subject to the input of a team of godly advisors. (Additionally, someone making such a choice to carefully accumulate should make every effort to give at least a sizeable fraction of their ongoing gains away, to train the heart toward generosity.)

For a business owner who spends according to their Spending Finish Line from the business proceeds, reinvests appropriately for growth, and views all upside from that point as belonging to God for Kingdom work, we believe the size of the business as it relates to personal net worth does not necessarily present a problem. It is possible to go the extra mile, however, and follow in the footsteps of Alan Barnhart, who gave his entire $250 million company away to a charitable trust while retaining voting control. R. G. LeTourneau, as a counterpoint, retained personal ownership of his company but gave 90 percent of his income (derived from the company) away. For those who face these types of challenges, we recommend first and foremost a policy of radical financial transparency with a team of accountability partners. Will Pope told us that, at first, he would "rather walk down the street naked" than share all of his finances, but that once he had done so the sense of freedom and peace gained was remarkable.

For a Closer Look . . .

Alan Barnhart has inspired a tremendous wave of generosity by sharing his story of faithfulness to God's word. A handful of business leaders have even followed his radical example in recent years, with the help of the National Christian Foundation, giving their entire companies away.

Listen to Alan tell his story in this 17-minute video, "God Owns Our Business," at GodandMoney.net/resources.

CONCLUSION TO CHAPTER SEVEN

By attaching savings goals to our calling and needs for provision in life, we can establish overall finish lines, or net worth cutoff points at which there is no further need for wealth accumulation. We found this to be a very freeing idea!

We believe organizing thoughts and plans for our stewardship into a personal Generosity Covenant is a valuable exercise for managing giving in the long run. Examples follow at the end of Chapter Eight. We also have a spreadsheet designed to calculate finish lines under a variety of scenarios, which is available for download on our website GodandMoney.net.

We would like to make one final note regarding possessions. We noted in the previous chapter that spending and giving should begin to blur in a generously lived life. The same is true for our savings or possessions. The entirety of our lives should belong to Jesus, and this includes all of our consumption and all of our wealth. Hence, your car and your house should be always, 100 percent available to bless your church and others, even though they are "yours." A Christian who follows our framework with absolute precision, yet fails to be hospitable or welcoming, has likely not yet grasped the essence of generosity!

FRAMEWORK SUMMARY FOR CHAPTERS SIX AND SEVEN

"I feel that my major calling in life is to fund ministry. I go to work every day with the motivation of making as much money as I can so that I can give more to advance the Gospel and especially the local church."
—Survey Response

First, we recommend choosing the lowest spending level that can responsibly take care of your family's needs and provide for fully realizing the "human vocation" of each family member. This advice is common to both a Christian worldview and a secular personal finance lens—the lower your consumption, the more excess cash you have every year. As your income grows, your consumption should grow at a slower pace, allowing saving and giving to take a larger cut of your paycheck. Eventually, once your spending reaches a level you are happy with as a steward of the income God has blessed you with, it stops growing altogether, with all excess income being allocated toward saving and giving. We think a reasonable upper limit on spending is around $100,000 to $150,000 per year, for a moderately sized family in a city with typical cost-of-living. Our case studies include those who have set limits for themselves lower than this range (the Samuels) and higher than this range (Will Pope), all of whom appear to be living fully in the Servant mindset. For a large family living in a high-cost metropolis like San Francisco or New York City, the upper bound could be materially higher.

We propose a "20 Percent Test" to determine whether your lifestyle is appropriate and God-honoring. Take your overall monthly spending level and ask yourself the two following questions.

- First, if you increased spending by 20 percent, what would you add to your lifestyle? Are these new additions worthwhile, enhancing your ability to live out your calling and to honor God? Are they worth allocating funds to, when the same funds could be saved up or given to build Christ's Kingdom?

- Second, if you cut spending by 20 percent, what would you eliminate? Would keeping these things be worthwhile by the standard stated above?

This exercise may require careful consideration. Take some time to sit down and write out the implications; we believe that careful evaluation of one's budget is a required act of sound stewardship.

After the consumption decision has been made, allocate your excess cash with prayerful wisdom, taking into consideration your stage of wealth accumulation, the needs of your church community, and your personal desires to give. Early in life, saving may take priority as debts are eliminated. As you move from being a debtor to an investor, your focus should shift toward more substantial levels of giving. As you reach The Basics and possibly approach financial independence, giving should absolutely take center stage, so that by the time you reach your personally established Personal Wealth Finish Line, your generosity can overflow from a generous and thankful heart.

We hope that it goes without saying that each person's giving plans should be open to the guidance of the Holy Spirit. If someone is led to give a huge amount early on, this framework should not stand in the way.

Wealth Finish Lines are dependent upon personal goals and choices, but we suggest that the cap for the vast majority of families could be in the single-digit millions. Our personal opinion is that most families can clearly use a wealth of at least one million dollars for reasonable purposes of provision, while a large family in an expensive city could probably do just fine with $10 million or less in ultimate wealth. These cases bracket the range in which you can find probably yourself.[141] (These values merely represent our opinion and should be taken as such. The number for your family, based on a variety of inputs and assumptions, can be estimated using our spreadsheet tool and/or through your own calculations or consultations with an advisor.)

---

141   This range represents roughly 20 to 200 times the median family income.

We are keenly aware that this vision of wealth is entirely counter-cultural. So was Jesus. When a Spender dreams of wealth, they may think of larger custom homes, new toys, and exotic vacations. Savers, by contrast, might think of building lasting family wealth, or earning early retirement and greater security. Servants, however, begin with thankfulness for material blessings, then naturally watch their thoughts drift to the wonderful impact they could have on their church, financing missionaries, and lifting the spirits of the poor.

We can always find ways to justify higher spending and higher accumulation of wealth. The purpose of this biblically based framework is to carefully consider, "How much is enough?" If we let the Holy Spirit lead us in this area the impact could be tremendous, both in terms of our personal growth and in blessings to the body of Christ.

The figure below demonstrates a wealth hierarchy that corresponds to the Saving Framework.

Figure 5: Wealth Hierarchy

All Excess Given Away!
Renunciation of endless accumulation

Luxuries: Financial Independence, Business Equity, Other Desires?
High levels of giving as wealth builds

The Basics: Home Ownership, Personal Retirement, and Education of Children
Balanced giving and saving as family needs are met

Elimination of Consumer Debts
Focus on saving as debts are paid; moderated giving

In closing this chapter, we give the final word to an anonymous survey respondent, who we believe captured the tensions of stewardship and the call to give in a beautiful way:

> *Our wealth is not really ours; it is something over which we are stewards. It is also a danger to our faith; a theme throughout Scripture is the spiritual danger rich people face. As such, we must be willing, as Jesus counseled the rich man, to give away all we have to the poor. . . . This is difficult because, as humans, we always want more and we tend to think that if we just had a little more, then we could give away the rest. We must recognize and fight against this tendency of planning to give at a later date rather than giving now from what we have.*
>
> *We also must fight against the temptation to believe that we have somehow been bestowed this wealth because we deserve it; that is a spiritual danger most profound. It is not something we deserve, it is something with which we have been entrusted and we need to use it to change the world, not to make ourselves more comfortable.*

CHAPTER EIGHT

Serving—Investing in Eternity Through Giving

*"You're not gonna hear, 'Well done,
good and faithful investor.'"*
—Al Mueller, President of Excellence in Giving

*"God could call you to die for your faith,
so how big of a deal is your 401k, really?"*
—Former business leader, now serving as a missionary overseas. (He drew down his
retirement savings to fund his ministry.)

Edward Heath jolted awake, immediately noticing his clammy hands and the nervous knot in his stomach. Was he about to make the biggest mistake of his life? He glanced over his peacefully sleeping wife, Katherine, at the clock and saw that it was 3:30 a.m. He had a few more hours to sleep but his mind was racing, so he got up and silently walked out of the room and sat down, instinctively opening the Bible app on his iPhone.

One Hundred Thousand Dollars. Many people save their entire lives yet barely reach that number in liquid wealth. Now in his early 30s, Edward was making good money in real-estate finance, but before he finished business school he had been serving as a

Naval Officer, which is not exactly the highest paying job around. Accumulating wealth was a new game for him and Katherine, and $100,000 was a big portion of their net worth. Would giving such a huge gift be nothing but stupidity? Could generosity be taken too far?

"First Kings 17." Edward had heard the Holy Spirit speak to him before, but this felt especially clear. He wracked his brain, trying to figure out whether he knew the passage. Nothing. Either his mind had picked a random chapter from nowhere, or this really was the Holy Spirit. Time to read. Edward worked through the passage, in which the widow feeds Elijah her last bit of bread and oil, but the stock is miraculously replenished. After this experience, Elijah defeats the prophets of Baal in the showdown on Mt. Carmel.

Edward felt the Lord's voice speaking to his heart: "I didn't need the widow's flour to feed my prophet, just like I don't need your sacrificial gift of money. The gift is for your benefit. I am giving you the privilege and opportunity to partner with me to slay the gods of pride and greed in your life and in your community, like the false prophets of Baal were slain on Mt. Carmel."

With this incredible message of reassurance, a sense of relief came over Edward. He thought back to how he had gotten to this point in his life. Married at 22, he and Katherine had always tithed and several times had been led to give additional big gifts. Tithing was never a stretch even though, back then, they were living on his $62,000 salary as a Naval Officer and her $30,000 salary at a staffing firm. Soon after their wedding, God decided to test their hearts and they each felt the urge to write a $5,000 check. This was a huge commitment, but they followed through and blessed their local church, experiencing an overwhelming joy at being able to contribute such a big number to God's work.

One year later the strong urge returned, but this time the number they had in mind was $10,000. With Katherine now working as an accounting professional their total income was higher, but the gift was proportionally huge nonetheless. Believing God was calling them to big giving, and feeling led by the Holy Spirit, they had written one more $10,000 check right after Edward had applied to Harvard Business School, a "pre-tithe, of sorts, on the $100,000 in tuition it would cost if we got in."

As they gave these big, sacrificial gifts, the Heaths had gained an appetite and an ambition for giving, but $100,000 was literally a whole new order of magnitude. Their income was definitely not 10 times higher than when they had given $10,000. Edward had felt led to this gift weeks before, but withheld his feeling from Katherine out of fear she would react badly to the idea. When the news finally broke between them, she revealed that she had been hiding the same exact number, for the same reason! Despite this double-confirmation, their nervousness about the gift was understandable. Even after their experiences of receiving God's grace and blessings in the aftermath of their previous gifts, stepping their generosity up a notch was a big challenge to their all-too-human desire for security and wealth-building.

Once they confirmed they each wanted to move ahead, the Heaths spent a few weeks in prayer asking God how to allocate the gift. They wanted to be strategic about such a large commitment and make the most of the gift. They solidified a plan to give 20 percent to their church, establishing a scholarship program for the church's overseas orphanage. Tuition, Katherine discovered, was only $1,500 per year at the nearby university, and many of the church's orphans could not afford the fees after aging out of the orphan homes. Considering their own giving passions, this was a perfect fit. Another 50 percent of the gift would go toward the church's unallocated budget. The Heath's felt that the Lord had given them discretion over the final 30 percent, which they allocated among causes and ministries that they believed in.

Edward and Katherine look back on this milestone gift as the high point of their long giving journey, so far. However, they have continued ambitions for giving on a bigger scale, and dream of the day when God will enable them to write a one million dollar check—another order of magnitude difference! Their lifestyle has remained relatively stable given their aggressive giving patterns. As their income increases, their giving scales alongside it. Indeed, their careers continue to thrive, with Katherine now the Controller of a Private Equity firm and Edward closing more and more deals as a real-estate finance professional, but their increased income has gone more toward giving than anything else.

They typify the Servant mentality with their money, and giving clearly takes priority over aggressive saving or spending. At his church, Edward has recently helped establish a stewardship ministry consisting of people who want to grow their spiritual gift of giving.

You may recall my (John) penchant for being a Saver. To me, the Heath family's story was an inexplicable anomaly within my worldview of money. How could you give away $100,000 when you aren't done saving for retirement, or college for your kids? They clearly are oriented 100 percent around the Servant mindset. Their giving story, however, appealed to me on another level. The details of their gift, practically speaking, feel like a model to be followed.

After speaking with the Heaths and our other case studies, we asked ourselves what the commonalities were around how people actually give well. Once we decide to up the ante in our financial generosity, what are the nuts and bolts of doing so in the right way? As we reflected on their story and our other case studies, some common characteristics emerged. We have come to believe that there are three key criteria we see as best practices for getting the giving game right.

- First, gifts must be **Gospel-centered**. If not, they lose their eternal value.

- Second, great gifts are **aligned with the giver's personal ministry calling**. Why not give our money to the same place we give our time and talent, where we have strong relationships, to an area where God has called and enabled us to make a difference?

- And finally, giving is best when it is done with **maximum effectiveness**. This is a self-evident statement, but it's often hard to work out in practice.

We believe that the best giving manages to satisfy all three of these key criteria.

For the Heaths' story, it's clear to see how all three criteria were met. They gave to their local church and to Christian orphan care, so the Gospel-centered criterion is clearly satisfied. They have a heart for the poor and dispossessed, meaning that their personal ministry calling was met. Finally, given the low tuition rates in the country of sponsorship, paying the tuition of an orphan is a very low-cost investment in a future leader. Also, the church had already invested in the "sunk cost" of raising each child for years, so the marginal investment to help them gain valuable skills for life had a potentially large return on investment!

As we dug in to the giving stories of our case studies, we also read books in the field and interviewed professionals working in the effective philanthropy space. In this section we will walk through our journey of learning on these three critical criteria, exploring best practices and inspiring examples as we go.

How Should We Then Give? The Three Giving Goals

Gospel-Centered

> *"Finding armies of people to volunteer one Saturday per year to paint dilapidated houses is easy. Finding people to love the people, day in and day out, who live in those houses is extremely difficult."*
>
> —When Helping Hurts[142]

We recognized that Brandon Fremont's income level likely meant that he was solicited often for money. We were eager to find out how he handles these situations and asked if he writes "little" checks for a thousand dollars to appease secular non-profits. We were curious to hear Brandon's answer to this, given his intense and contagious focus on Scripture as the guide for our actions as Christ-followers.

He responded quickly with a story. Recently, the teenage daughter of one of his friends had sent a letter asking for his support to do some humanitarian work in Central America. It was a secular organization aiming to help alleviate some material suffering that was ongoing in the region. Brandon's instinct was to say no, and gently explain that he was fully committed with his giving to other causes. But then he paused and thought it over. "Would I pay $100 to have someone read a letter in which I lay out the hope of the Gospel? Yes, all day long."

---

142   Corbett, Steve and Fikkert, Brian, *When Helping Hurts* (Chicago: Moody Publishers)

Brandon wrote out a check for $100 and attached a letter, explaining that he was very grateful for the work this woman intended to do. However, he included the following: "Clean water, food, and shelter are great things. But everyone is going to meet the Lord of the universe when they die, and I want my giving to help people have the right answer when that happens, in addition to taking care of those other needs." He humbly suggested that she consider this eternal perspective in her future work, as she continued striving to make the world a better place. This is now Brandon's regular habit. He views it as a $50 or $100 fee (insignificant in the scheme of his overall giving budget) to have someone read the Gospel, presented in a letter, who probably would never otherwise do so.

Brandon's dogged focus on the Gospel of Jesus Christ above all else reflects his understanding of the Word of God. We are indeed called to address material needs where we find them, but to do so in a strictly humanitarian sense, devoid of the Gospel, is to leave out the greatest cause for hope that we have to offer. In order to gain perspective on this, we turned to the Scriptures and also to a leading and recent book on Christian aid ministry, *When Helping Hurts*.

Three anchor verses in Scripture help define our call to serve the world in the name of Christ.

- First, Jesus famously launched His ministry in Luke 4:18-19: "The Spirit of the Lord is upon me, because He has anointed me to proclaim good news to the poor. He has sent me to proclaim liberty to the captives and recovering of sight to the blind, to set at liberty those who are oppressed, to proclaim the year of the Lord's favor." Jesus had a clear focus on reaching people with deep and desperate needs.

- Second, Paul writes in 2 Corinthians 5:18, "All this is from God, who through Christ reconciled us to Himself and gave us the ministry of reconciliation."

- Finally, Jesus left His followers with the Great Commission before He ascended to heaven. Matthew 28:19-20 states, "Go therefore and make disciples of all nations, baptizing them in the name of the Father and of the Son and of the Holy Spirit, teaching them to observe all that I have commanded you."

We therefore are ministers to this broken world, in the tradition of Christ, with the task of providing reconciliation. As we reach out to the neediest people in the world, working to bring reconciliation to all areas of their lives, we first and foremost should teach them to be disciples of Jesus. *When Helping Hurts* spends some time unpacking what it means, tactically, to bring reconciliation. In short, our giving should seek to redeem both individual people and the broader systems that people live within. Exclusively working to bring personal salvation may leave institutional injustice unresolved, while working purely for social justice without addressing personal sin and salvation would be a ministry devoid of eternal significance. We must do both.

Evangelical giving in the modern age may lean too far to the personal, individualistic side of this balance, avoiding the need to tackle lingering issues of injustice in our society. In Isaiah 58 God lambastes the people of Israel. Why was the Lord angry? As the authors of *When Helping Hurts* reflect, "These folks were faithfully going to church each Sunday, attending midweek prayer meeting, going on the annual church retreat, and singing contemporary praise music. But God was disgusted with them . . . over [their] failure to care for the poor and the oppressed. He wanted His people to 'loose the chains of injustice.'"[143]

---

143   Ibid, 39

Injustice is often most at work in communities and social subgroups that are invisible to those of us blessed with higher incomes. For us (John and Greg), it was a terrifying thought to apply the 58th chapter of Isaiah to our own lives, in which we had perhaps done far too little to break the chains of injustice which are all too powerful even in the 21st century.

Extending this thought, it is easy for us to sponsor someone's summer camp within our middle-class to upper-class churches, because the need is visible and we have relationships there. But, we found ourselves asking, what about poorer youth who live across town, who are not in a youth group and have never been to a summer camp? Maybe faithfully giving to our churches, but ignoring the plight of the less fortunate, is simply unacceptable? "Woe to you, scribes and Pharisees, hypocrites! For you tithe mint and dill and cumin, and have neglected the weightier matters of the law: justice and mercy and faithfulness. These you ought to have done, without neglecting the others" (Matthew 23:23). As Jesus points out, simply giving is not enough. We are called to bring justice and mercy to where they are needed! It is worth quoting from *When Helping Hurts* again:

> *What happens when society crams historically oppressed, uneducated, unemployed, and relatively young human beings into high-rise buildings; takes away their leaders; provides them with inferior education, health care, and employment systems; and then pays them not to work? Is it really that surprising that we see out-of-wedlock pregnancies, broken families, violent crimes, and drug trafficking?*

Our ministry calling is to reach into this world—broken institutions and broken lives—and seek to provide the healing that only

Christ can bring. As we studied Scripture, we became increasingly convinced that this means reaching out to help the poor and the marginalized. Helping our high-income church to construct a new wing or retreat center is wonderful, but we became convinced that if we did this while ignoring the neediest in our society, we would be entering some dangerous territory in the eyes of God.

If we are followers of Jesus, our giving must be aligned with the imperatives of Scripture. Scripture tells us clearly to make disciples of Christ, and to care for "the least of these" in the world. If Jesus were here with us in 21ˢᵗ century America, we conjecture that He would be often spotted out among the dispossessed, providing a call to repentance and healing, spending many of his days in Section 8 high-rises. Even if we live and work solely within high-income geographies, through our charitable giving we have the opportunity to further Christ's ministry, bringing healing in His name everywhere from the ends of the earth, to the other side of our hometown.

ALIGNMENT WITH PERSONAL MINISTRY CALLING

Remember Will Pope, sitting in the café in San Jose and realizing his true calling was to do what God had prepared him for? To go back home to earn money and give to the work of God from his earnings? Well, when he and his wife, Rachel, physically left Central America, their hearts remained in the developing world. Rachel's passion for raising up Christian leaders in emerging economies has proved infectious to Will and has been the dynamo behind their giving efforts for over 20 years.

Their ministry, funded almost exclusively from his own donations, provides university scholarships to students in poorer countries. The typical student comes from a background of living on as little as two dollars per day. They all commit to serve a social or Christian organization for the duration of their studies, while being mentored under the wing of a local ministry partner. The program has sponsored hundreds of students through college and continues to grow. As Will and Rachel have deepened their expertise and partnered with organizations in multiple countries around the world to expand the program, its effectiveness has increased. Since we (John and Greg) each have young children, we dream of putting a few of our own children through college. Will and Rachel, meanwhile, are putting hundreds of other people's children through college! (And as for taking credit? You won't find their last name on the associated foundation.)

One partner of the ministry, a country director for a local Christian organization, had this to say: "It [not only gave] people access to go to University, but it has saved people from death: spiritually, socially, and economically." While there is no future service commitment for program participants, this partner reported that several of his staff positions were filled by graduates of the program, eager to give back.

Will's focus, commitment, and long-term vision for his ministry foundation is inspirational, but also almost intimidating. Here I am, a relatively rich American with significant future resources to bring to bear on the problems of the world, and I haven't even chosen a focus yet! I kind of want to help solve the sex trafficking issue, definitely care a lot about orphans, and would also like to maybe sponsor a missionary. But of course, I should give to my local church too. How can I ever get from here to where Will is?

Will's story and others like it demonstrate the power of aligning one's personal ministry calling, based on skills, abilities, and passions, with financial giving. This is how one can really step into Servant territory! When we take on a piece of God's mission on the earth, it is only natural to apply every resource we have, including money, toward advancing that mission. This can help our giving to come alive, energizing us rather than feeling like a line item expense to be paid.

Broadly speaking, we know that the Body of Christ should minister to all manifestations of brokenness while sharing the gospel, but individually our callings may diverge widely. From our overarching call to the ministry of reconciliation, we must individually consider our gifts, our financial circumstances, local needs, and what giving opportunities are available in forming a personal vision for our giving. While some people have an immediate sense for what moves their heart and where they want to give, others (including me, John) may have several interests or feel moved by a wide variety of causes. Randy Alcorn suggests in *The Treasure Principle* that, if you lack a heart for something specific, the first step to gain passion is simply starting to give![144]

From personal experience, however, just cutting a check is not enough. We've all heard sermons encouraging us to use our three *T*'s—Time, Talent, and Treasure—to advance the Gospel. When all three are in alignment, working toward the same cause, the sum can be much more than the parts. My own personal mistake has been that I have simply cut checks, sponsoring an orphan home for the past three years, but have not formed any real connection with it. Through talking with our case studies and speaking with experts, I came to realize that I needed to gain better overall alignment and focus in my giving strategy.

I spoke with Grace Nicolette of the Center for Effective Philanthropy, and asked her about this issue. "Spreading things around feels right, because you love people, have a heart for their work, and enjoy giving to their causes. But focusing really has

---

144   Alcorn, Randy. *The Treasure Principle*, 44.

more power." *Give Smart*[145] agrees, arguing that peanut-butter philanthropy, by which a small number of dollars are thrown at a large number of causes, dilutes the potential impact that a donor could have if they focused more narrowly. While broad giving will likely produce average results, developing specialized abilities for a small number of specific causes could generate superior impact over the long-term. Thinking back to our first-year MBA course on business strategy, we learned something similar: doing one thing well makes you a real competitor. Doing a dozen things halfway decently makes you bankrupt.

Specialization, then, can have immense value for earning outsize "returns" on your giving dollars. While it is easy to say that you want to "do good" or "spread the gospel," such phrases aren't that useful in this context. If you're stuck, like me, there are a few things we can try.

- First, let's pray and ask God to put a calling on our hearts as we walk forward in this area of life.

- Second, let's seek wisdom from trusted Christian friends who we respect, our church, and/or our families.

- Third, let's set aside time to reflect and read on topics that might interest us.

- Finally, it will be important to avoid paralysis. Let's learn as we go, rather than studying the issue to death.

I've come to peace with the fact that it may take me a year, or two, or five, to figure out this "calling" thing. That's OK—I trust in the Lord's grace as I walk this out with my wife and family! In *Give Smart*, the authors point out that failure to specialize is often "not

---

145   Tierney, Thomas J. and Fleischman, Joel L, *Give Smart* (New York: Public Affairs)

so much a question of making a 'wrong' choice as it is of failing to make a choice in the first place." That's a failure I want to avoid.

As a final note here, it may be worth considering something addressed in *When Helping Hurts*.[146] The authors point out that while there are many ways to do good through giving, there are also a few ways to do harm. Inappropriate relief work can enable dependency in the served population, meaning that donated dollars are actually making the world worse off! There are, the authors explain, three types of aid that can be given: relief, rehabilitation, and development. Relief is provided when someone's urgent, acute problem is solved by giving. Think of natural disasters, medical emergencies, forced bondage, etc. Rehabilitation comes after relief, and involves helping someone attain the status in life they had before the acute disaster struck. Development is a longer-term journey of growth that helps someone move out of chronic brokenness and address deeply rooted issues in their life. Development, the authors argue, is the hardest and also the most desperately needed form of ministry in the world. However, an outsized portion of charitable giving goes straight to relief. Why the mismatch?

Relief sells, relief is (relatively) easy, and relief is measurable. Throw up a picture of an earthquake-ravaged city, and the money pours in. It's a powerful emotional stimulus to see images of disaster and they rightly stir our hearts. It is much easier to buy a homeless person a meal than it is to say, "Brother, how can I walk alongside you for the next six months in a way that would allow you to break free of any sinful behavior patterns in your life, gain employable skills, and get on a path to a better future?" And finally, a food bank can easily measure short-term impact: "Five dollars can feed a family tonight!" Efforts to provide development,

---

146   Corbett and Fikkert, *When Helping Hurts*

however, are more difficult to track. Emotional breakthroughs, spiritual healing, and incremental job skills are worthy results, but cannot be so easily traced to financial inputs.

Given these realities, there may be an opportunity to add significant value in the realm of development, since so many people are already focused on relief. For the finance-oriented readers, development is "under-priced," so the potential returns are huge for an astute "investor!" As the authors point out, "One of the biggest mistakes that North American churches make—by far—is in applying relief in situations in which rehabilitation or development is the appropriate intervention."

Will Pope's scholarship program and ministry is solidly a developmental effort, oriented toward the long-term future of the students he sponsors and the societies they live within, advancing the Gospel of Christ. How much better this is than simply flying a team in, building them a little house, and flying back out again! Helping your church establish a development-oriented giving program may be one way you could strive to make a strategic impact on the world. We highly recommend *When Helping Hurts* for further study in this area; the book contains myriad strategies and ministry recommendations along these lines.

Ideally, we can "put our money where our ministry is" on the earth. Sometimes, we'll undoubtedly just write checks. As we grow up as believers, though, let's strive to find our own niche in which we can make an outsized impact for God's Kingdom by fully aligning our Time, Talent, and Treasure.

Maximum Effectiveness

"Generosity alone is rarely sufficient if you aspire to leave a legacy of exceptional results."
—Give Smart

"It's going to cost how much each time we use the facility? Wow, that's higher than last time we talked. OK, I'll see what I can do." Our friend hung up the phone and scratched his chin, deep in thought. He had helped raise money for a nonprofit organization in a local town that benefited hundreds, even thousands of people on a regular basis. However, costs were continually an issue, because the large gatherings hosted by the organization were forced to use the biggest venue around, as it was the only place nearby that could host a group of their size. He began to wonder if there was a better way to tackle the problem than simply asking donors for additional funds to support the program.

Working with some of his contacts and connections, he formed a small team that worked together to find a creative solution for the next several months. After crossing over a pile of red tape and forging many new relationships along the way, this team and the relevant government officials eventually agreed that the use of the facility was a worthy public cause. With the support of everyone involved, the fee was dropped to a nominal figure that simply covered the cost of utilities and cleaning.

This story demonstrates the power of how non-financial factors can take giving effectiveness to the next level. Rather than just raising more money to keep the program going, our friend engaged his network, his abilities, and his creativity to unlock value for the public and for the ministry! Aligning time, talent, and treasure is the first and best way to ensure effective giving success. Just like debt on a business can boost equity returns, applying your time and abilities can leverage giving dollars to have maximum impact.

Hearing so many exciting giving stories in recent months has made me realize that I have mostly measured my family's giving by a simple percent-of-income total. This seems to be common among my friends as well. We fail to measure return on investment, out of the assumption that our church, or the charity we support, will wisely manage the funds. I check portfolio balances quite often, eager to ensure that I'm capturing the market's advances. Conversely, however, I wash my hands of all responsibility or involvement once a giving check is written. This simplistic view has deprived the Kingdom of God of my full talents, and is something I deeply hope to improve on as I move forward. We certainly don't need to nit-pick every dime that our church spends, or criticize every line item on a charity's budget. Rather, watching giving veterans has shown me that we should bring our whole suite of abilities and knowledge to the charitable giving process, ensuring before God that we maximize the Kingdom-utility of the dollars He allows to pass through our hands.

In investing, returns are captured and reported as a return-on-investment (ROI). This is easy and simple, because invested dollars beget more dollars. Performance is a cold, hard fact that is easy to measure and report. In giving, measurement is vastly more difficult, but that doesn't mean the task should be avoided. Let's maximize souls-saved per dollar, emotional-healing per dollar, poverty-alleviated per dollar, etc., as our case studies have done in their own lives. We will refer to this notion of effectiveness as Kingdom Return-on-Investment, or K_{ROI}. It occurred to me through the writing of this book that I had spent my entire life striving eagerly for maximum financial returns through reading, coursework, and professional skill-building, but had never gone much further than placing a check in an offering plate when it came to thinking about K_{ROI}.

Jesus seems to encourage mindfulness around this issue of effectiveness based upon a couple of examples from his ministry. First, he left his hometown when his message was not well-received (Mark 6:4), and second, he instructed his disciples to shake the dust from their feet and leave any place where their message was not welcome (Matthew 10:14). Implicitly, he encouraged maximizing the return on invested time in ministry, by giving more time to places where the Gospel was accepted. His instructions ensure the highest "souls saved per hour of ministry" ratio, and have helped many believers avoid tossing pearls to swine.

Similarly, Paul regularly pointed to results in his own ministry track record as evidence of his faithfulness as a steward of the message and burden God had entrusted him with on the road to Damascus. He didn't just say that he cared a lot, or that he had good intentions . . . he pointed to tangible results, and the hard work that drove them.[147] The same logic should apply to financial giving in the Christian world. Without good stewardship we could find ourselves giving to ineffective ministries for years on end without even knowing it!

A concept from finance that may be useful here is the notion of risk-adjusted returns. When taking higher risks, failure becomes more of a possibility, but the upside also becomes much greater. Our Board of Directors for Life is investing in a high-risk, high-chance-of-failure project to advance the Gospel. There may be a 50 percent chance of total failure—we could "lose" our money. But, if successful the harvest would be tremendous.

147　"To ensure that his labor was worthwhile and not in vain, [his] work to advance the gospel was measured by the increase in the number of believers and in the growth in the fruit of the spirit in the believers (1 Thess. 2:1; 3:5). In fact, the health of the church was a measure of the success of his work. Paul wrote that he was laboring "so that in the day of Christ I may be proud that I did not run in vain or labor in vain" (Phil. 2:16). —David Kotter, *Working for the Glory of God.* PhD dissertation. Southern Baptist Theological Seminary, May 2015

Hosting a church small group is lower risk, and modest in returns. The probability of success is very high—everyone will probably grow in fellowship and seek the Lord together, which is great. However, it's also unlikely that tens of thousands of people will be fed, clothed, or come to know Jesus as Savior. When making Kingdom investments, we must keep in mind the risk of failure, our own risk tolerance, and our sense of calling. Local, lower-risk ventures are akin to purchasing certificates-of-deposit or bonds, and they have a valid place in our Kingdom-investing portfolio.

Highly risky, globally oriented giving to frontier missions, etc., is akin to investing in an early-stage startup. Astute investors know they may lose it all, but they accept this risk because of the potential for enormous benefits. We hope to invest in both "bonds" and in "startups" in our giving careers, and intend to keep the risk/return framework in mind in each circumstance.

My own immediate thought at this point in the journey was to make use of online charity-screening tools to figure out effectiveness, eliminating the need for further personal research. However, industry experts I spoke with quickly pointed out that these rating tools only scratch the surface. Charity Navigator, for example, is a well-known rating agency that gives out an overall zero to four star rating based on a ministry's Financial Performance and Accountability. Understanding these categories is necessary but not sufficient. Imagine a charity that gives away $100 bills to help impoverished people purchase sports cars. Such an organization could be highly efficient and highly transparent, but a four-star rating on these dimensions fails to show us that the core strategy of the ministry is terrible! Similarly, a charity with an effective, fully staffed management team might receive poor scores based on their high overhead levels, even if the team is driving impressive results on the ground. It is up to the person giving the money to be aware of these nuances.

If our local church is the "default" option for giving, then, it looks like the burden of proof needed for us to give somewhere else is going to be relatively high. If we give outside the church, we assume responsibility for ensuring we pick a good charity or a mission that we are especially confident in (think of Will Pope's passion for third-world college scholarships). The local church is a critical foundation for all Kingdom work, providing a nurturing home for spiritual growth and maturity in every community. Each component of the Christian ministry ecosystem has unique value, but the local church is a bedrock foundation that should never be neglected financially. Brandon Fremont and his accountability group go so far as to audit each other's giving trends—if someone begins giving less than 60 percent of their total gifts to the local church, the group treats it as a flag for further discussion.

While we recognize that there are some wonderful opportunities to give to parachurch organizations, overseas missions, and humanitarian development, doing so to the neglect of the local church would be a tragedy. We believe that this God-ordained institution is worthy of strong financial backing. As Al Mueller, President of Excellence in Giving, puts it, "If you can't trust them with your money, why are you comfortable trusting them with your salvation?"

Another benefit of giving locally to your church is the sunk cost of your time and relationships there. You have already done half of the due-diligence work just by going every Sunday and reading the bulletin!

When churches are laser-focused on their mission to reach the world, it can really empower giving to take off to new heights. I recently spoke with Pastor David Self of Houston's First Baptist Church, in an attempt to learn how their focused, mission-oriented giving campaign for 2013 and 2014 brought in $30 million over and above the previous giving trend observed in the church! Nearly half of all givers in this two-year period were first-time donors to the church. I asked Pastor Self what had people so excited.

In short, the church provided an opportunity to become a part of a bigger mission, and made this opportunity crystal clear to those who gave. As Pastor Self explained, "the outward focus of the church . . . [became] the uniting force for generosity in the community. When the church casts a vision, people are awakened to the opportunity. It's all about the outreach, the mission." The messaging within the campaign made it clear that any contributions would go 100 percent toward missions: to the city of Houston, the nation of America, and the broader world.

Today, roughly half of this church's overall budget is missional. We believe this is an inspiring example of how a church can awaken generosity among its congregation, which enables a new missional focus within the budget, which then fuels further giving. It's a life-giving virtuous cycle. While many church members may not take the time to personally seek out their giving passions, if the church casts a compelling vision, these members can be inspired to jump on board. The Lead Pastor, Gregg Matte, is releasing a book on all that they have learned called *Unstoppable Gospel*, which will be available by the time you're reading this. We can't wait to get our hands on it.

If you have doubts that your church is providing maximum K_{ROI}, perhaps there is a chance to get constructively involved in helping shape the direction of ministry activities. It is easy to criticize; it is harder but more fruitful to get engaged and provide help, to the extent your church's leadership team is receptive. Simply changing churches is the easy way out, and is probably the worst way to resolve the issue. The church you leave is then deprived of your God-given talents in stewardship. No pastor or team of staff is perfect, but we should give grace for their efforts to faithfully lead God's people. By approaching the issue with humility, respect, and with a willingness to learn, we can leave a productive and helpful legacy in our church's stewardship of the resources entrusted to it.

When giving outside the local church, good due-diligence is even more critical, given that we may not know anything about the charity before writing a check. No one would invest in a mutual fund just because it holds stocks and bonds, because this fact alone tells us nothing of the strategy, fee structure, etc. within the fund. Neither should we give to a charity simply because it does Christian work. The charity you have heard of, or the one your friend gives to, may or may not be the most effective in its field, and may or may not align with your own personal vision.

One resource we'd like to highlight that can help you perform a deeper analysis is Intelligent Philanthropy.[148] This is a service that screens charities in much greater detail than other online portals, charging a modest fee for membership. As a member, you can request an analysis of a charity of your choosing if one does not already exist. This is effectively an outsourced version of a foundation staff—a great solution for a busy professional with the desire to give effectively.

As we heard more and more stories, it dawned on us that the principles of effective giving should apply to all types of giving, not just tax-deductible donations to churches and charities. Giving to adult children or other relatives should be done in such a way as to enable development and independence, rather than fostering dependency or deepening a sense of shame at receiving aid. Does the recipient honor the Gospel? Are you personally eager to allocate your scarce resources to them? Do you think the gift will be effective over a short- and long-term horizon? Truth-seeking

---

148   www.intelligentphilanthropy.com

and an intentional cycle of learning will ensure that gifts within the family are serving a helpful purpose. Recall the lesson from *When Helping Hurts*—development is the ultimate goal, so applying relief willy-nilly will foster dependency rather than growth.

Brandon Fremont, who supports his elderly in-laws financially, found himself in a tough situation in the family domain recently. His deadbeat brother-in-law was always asking for money, but had yet to heed biblical advice about how to put his life on the right path, and was engaged in substance abuse. Brandon regularly had to turn him down, offering to help him in nonfinancial ways—help in which the brother-in-law was never interested.

A year ago, word leaked that Brandon's in-laws were giving their son money, unable to resist his continued supplications. Since Brandon was giving them money, he was frustrated to realize that he was now subsidizing an ungodly and dependent relationship. He had to gently confront his in-laws, telling them that his own financial support would be withdrawn if they did not cut off their son financially. Thankfully, the situation was resolved amicably, and with his subsidies withdrawn, it only took two weeks for the brother-in-law to agree to enter a rehab center. He has since given his life to Christ and has been sober for almost a year. Giving, whether to family, churches, or charities, must be done with a steward's eye toward effectiveness.

Finally, some of our interviewees shared that as you move through your life, there will probably be times when you "exit" your support of a ministry. Doing so with grace and openness is far better than suddenly pulling the plug. Just like incentivized early retirements are better than mass layoffs, easing into bad news can make life easier for everyone. When possible, communicating ahead of your decision and staging your withdrawal will give time for replacement funding to be located.

FINANCIAL MECHANICS OF GIVING

We want to close this discussion on effectiveness by addressing some tactical issues of giving. Keeping track of giving can become quite a challenge when you support multiple charities. Many we spoke to have found it convenient to give through a Donor-Advised Fund such as those offered by the National Christian Foundation. For a management fee of one percent per year or less (depending on assets) such a fund will hold your giving dollars until you provide instruction on where to give. You could write a check to your fund on the first of January and, for tax purposes, your charitable giving for the year would be finished. The actual disbursement of the money would come later, as you provide instruction.

Additionally, it is important to maximize the number of dollars that reach the church or charity you're supporting. It is prudent to fully utilize any corporate gift-matching program that your company makes available. At John's former company, Chevron, $10,000 per year in giving can be matched dollar-for-dollar. My wife and I leveraged this match to help fund Christian orphan care overseas for half-price!

Also, we generally recommend against using credit cards to give when it can be avoided, since the recipient organization may only receive approximately 97 to 98 percent of the donation due to fees. Discovering this fact was slightly painful for me, since I had high hopes for the amount of credit card points I could earn with my anticipated aggressive giving patterns in the future! I had to begrudgingly admit that a check is best, ensuring that 100 percent of the money goes right where it's intended.

It's worth briefly discussing taxes. While we often complain about facing taxes, Ron Blue likes to remind people that "taxes are symptomatic of provision." When we pay taxes, we can thank God for putting us in a place of abundant provision such that the IRS has taken an interest in us. That said, we ought to minimize our obligation with the tools available to us. Giving appreciated assets can be a major tax boon, because you get a write off for the appreciated value, without facing taxes on the capital gains. The lawyers at the National Christian Foundation are best-in-class for helping real estate, stock options, rare collectibles, etc., turn into tax-advantaged charitable giving for the Kingdom.

Also, Alan Barnhart recommends that high-income givers "join the 50 percent club as soon as humanly possible." The IRS allows you to exclude 50 percent charitable giving from your taxable income, and if you fail to capture this benefit in a given year, it is gone forever. Those tax dollars can't be recovered, and they could have gone to Kingdom causes. We know many wealthy believers who consider 50 percent giving to be their minimum baseline because of this logic.

Finally, if you are able to give five to six figures or more, it may be worth connecting with your church or charity to see whether you can have a strategic impact beyond simply contributing unallocated funds. With regard to charities, *Give Smart* points out that donors often overlook low-hanging fruit in the realm of overhead. Overhead is not evil in nonprofits; it is simply a neutral reality. A cash-strapped management team may greatly benefit from funding that enables them to construct a quality business plan, or hire a Chief Operating Officer, etc. Let's say you can invest $100,000 in central staffing and business planning capabilities, which will then allow a $10 million nonprofit to become five percent more efficient. Hypothetically, this investment would unlock $500,000 in value for a $100,000 investment—a very high K_{ROI}. Most people want every dime they give to go straight to program implementation, but by paying attention to every line item in a non-profit we may discover creative opportunities to add value.

We have covered a lot of ground. Perhaps enough ground to reveal our embarrassingly amateurish status in the domain of effective giving. Nonetheless, we have just scratched the surface of modern thinking on effective philanthropy. It would clearly be impossible to become an excellent financial Servant overnight. Like any other human skill, becoming a highly effective giver will be a lifelong journey, so we all might as well start accumulating our 10,000 hours now.[149]

If the goal is to run a marathon, a novice shouldn't be discouraged if they fail to reach 10 miles on their first training run. (Personally, I feel like the giver who is winded after a half-mile!) Similarly, we should let our giving be a journey of growth that begins with baby steps. Start with a Gospel-focus, then hone in on your personal areas of passion, and finally, strive to unlock maximum effectiveness. None of us will be a master of all three from day one, but we might as well jump in headfirst and get started.

A FINAL NOTE: WHEN SHOULD WE NOT GIVE?

Jesus clearly commands us to be generous. But is there ever a time we should *refrain* from giving? In Matthew 5:24 Jesus states, "Leave your gift there before the altar and go. First be reconciled to your brother, and then come and offer your gift." In Luke 11:42 Jesus admonishes the Pharisees: "But woe to you Pharisees! For you tithe mint and rue and every herb, but neglect justice and the love of God! These you ought to have done, without neglecting the others." These verses highlight the fact that while exhibiting generosity is a critical spiritual discipline, doing so is subordinate

---

149 Malcolm Gladwell's book *Outliers* posits the "10,000 hour rule," that great achievers are made, not born, through extreme amounts of practice and dedication.

to maintaining right relations with both God and our fellow man. God is relational, not transactional, and He wants our hearts to be right with Him and with others before receiving our gifts. We see in these passages that offering gifts to God while we have unrepentant sin in our lives actually dishonors Him. He wants us to be generous, but only for the right reasons—to honor Him and to serve others.

Putting the Framework to Work: Personal Generosity Covenants

After we developed the framework based on our research and observations of highly effective generous families, we recognized the need to distill our learnings down into an easy-to-reference document that our own families could live by. Signing our name on something also adds a level of commitment that simply thinking through various ideas does not. Thus, the Generosity Covenant was born. The Baumer and Cortines families sat down individually and wrote down the heart of our plans for financial Servanthood in Christ.

Greg and Alison's Generosity Covenant is shown on the following pages, providing what we hope will be a helpful example that other families might choose to follow. (Both this document and the Cortines family's Generosity Covenant are available on our website GodandMoney.net.) The beauty of the document is that it is a living and breathing expression of the joy that Christ has given us in our financial lives. Rather than a constrictive contract, it is a freeing way to express exactly where we stand before the Lord.

BAUMER FAMILY GENEROSITY COVENANT—2016

STEWARDSHIP PHILOSOPHY

"Yours, O LORD, is the greatness and the power and the glory and the victory and the majesty, for all that is in the heavens and in the earth is yours . . . Both riches and honor come from you, and you rule over all . . . And now we thank you, our God, and praise your glorious name."
—King David in 1 Chronicles 29

"Give, and it will be given to you. Good measure, pressed down, shaken together, running over, will be put into your lap. For with the measure you use it will be measured back to you."
—Jesus in Luke 6:38

"Their abundance of joy and their extreme poverty have overflowed in a wealth of generosity in their part. For they gave according to their means, as I can testify, and beyond their means, of their own accord, begging us earnestly for the favor of taking part in the relief of the saints."
—Paul in 2 Corinthians 8:2-4

"My service will be judged not by how much I have done, but by how much I could have done."
—A. W. Tozer

The Baumer family will honor the Lord with the wealth He gives us. We confess that God has sovereignty over our capacity to generate wealth and that all our possessions truly belong to God. We commit to serving as faithful stewards by actively and responsibly managing these blessings for His purposes. We will embrace a mindset of abundance toward our wealth, operating as Servants rather than as Savers or Spenders. We will live this way out of gratitude to Christ for His gift of salvation through grace.

SPENDING: STRATEGY AND FINISH LINE

We acknowledge all our resources truly belong to God. Therefore, we commit to thoughtfully considering the rationale behind our consumption choices. Our guiding principle will be to make all spending "live-giving." In practice, this means enjoying God's blessings of provision for a flourishing human life (e.g., investing in relationships, good food, travel, education, ministry, the arts, athletics, etc.) while living beneath our means and avoiding all non-mortgage/education debt.

Our current finish line will be $100,000 in cash spending per year. This is more than we could responsibly spend given our graduate school loans and the need to save for a down payment on a house, college tuition for our children, etc. We anticipate spending around $80,000 in 2016.

SAVING: STRATEGY AND FINISH LINE

We acknowledge God's sovereignty over our capacity to generate savings. If blessed with the ability to accumulate wealth, we will save until we can cover The Basics, which include a cash emergency fund, owning a comfortable home and reasonable vehicles, savings for college for our children, and being on-track with retirement savings. Accumulating wealth, however, will never come before a minimum baseline of giving (see next section).

We will strive to reduce net worth through aggressive giving if we ever have more than we need to obtain Financial Independence. If we are between The Basics and Financial Independence, we will make a judgment call whether to accumulate or disburse from our wealth in support of our Kingdom giving objectives with the counsel of wise Christian advisors.

In 2016, The Basics require about one million dollars for our family, whereas Financial Independence would require about four million dollars. We currently have graduate school debt in excess of $150,000 and are also saving for a down payment on a house, so we plan to accumulate savings in the near-term. (These values were calculated with the *God and Money* Personal Wealth Finish Line Spreadsheet.)

SERVING: STRATEGY

We will always give a minimum of 10 percent of pre-tax earnings, in any circumstance. In 2016, our goal is to balance the need to accumulate toward The Basics with a desire to give generously. We will target a pre-tax giving rate of 15 percent for 2016.

Our 2016 giving objectives include supporting:

- Our local church (approximately 60 percent of giving)

- Group giving: Scripture translation (approximately 20 percent)

- Local missions: InterVarsity, personal relationships with missions organizations and individual Kingdom workers (approximately 15 percent)

- Global missions: World Vision (approximately 5 percent)

We commit to fulfilling our role as God's stewards by attempting to maximize the K_{ROI} generated from our giving through prayer and personal investment of time and skills in addition to money.

We will seek to develop ambition toward our giving, founded in gratitude for Christ's gifts to us. This means pushing ourselves to give more and more in order to support God's Kingdom and experience His blessings.

TRANSPARENCY & ACCOUNTABILITY

We commit to radical transparency. Given the depravity of the human heart and the deceitfulness of riches, this is an area we are unwilling to handle alone.

We will send an annual stewardship report to our Board of Directors for Life and solicit feedback. Our 2015 report and plan has been delivered, and our 2016 version will go out by the end of the calendar year.

Any changes to our finish lines or strategies will be subject to review by our accountability partners.

OTHER CONSIDERATIONS

- Continue studying God's Word and pray regularly in order to gain wisdom with respect to our stewardship.

- Maintain life, disability, health insurance to avoid catastrophic loss.

- Involve our children in the giving process as they grow up.

COMMITMENT

This is a living document, to be maintained throughout our lives. We hereby commit to the principles above, for the glory of Christ our Savior!

_____,

Greg Baumer

_____,

Alison Baumer

PART III: FORWARD

CHAPTER NINE

Stewardship in Community

"We were surprised by how strong a testimony giving can be to non-believers, and even other Christians. People tell us, 'You guys are crazy!'"

—Brett and Christy Samuels

Living in fellowship with other Christians is critical to the development of our individual faith. "Therefore encourage one another and build one another up, just as you are doing" (1 Thessalonians 5:11). "Two are better than one, because they have a good reward for their toil. For if they fall, one will lift up his fellow . . . a threefold cord is not quickly broken" (Ecclesiastes 4:9, 12). "Iron sharpens iron, and one man sharpens another" (Proverbs 27:17).

Many churches are exceptional at fostering close-knit, encouraging, life-giving communities that support and nurture our individual faith. My wife and I (Greg) were blessed to be part of an incredible small group Bible study with five other couples during our four years living in Boston. We grew extremely close with these dear friends during that time. We shared together in life's adventures, both good and bad. We have celebrated job promotions and the births of beautiful children, and have prayed for healing from serious health complications and supported each other during difficult periods in our marriages. We ate together, served together, prayed together, even vacationed together!

Despite the closeness of our group, however, there is one topic we never discussed in four years: our finances. I know nothing about their faithfulness in stewardship, their spending and saving habits, or their vision for honoring God with their wealth and giving. Why is this? Given how important God clearly considers our management of money to be, why do we talk so little about it? Shira Boss, author of *Green With Envy*, calls it "the money taboo:"

> *The fact that [Christians] can't talk about our finances is getting us into trouble.... I interviewed a family who had gotten into nearly $100,000 of credit card debt and were driven into bankruptcy. They were too ashamed to tell any friends or family of their trauma. Even worse, they felt they couldn't confide in their pastor or any of the other couples in their close-knit weekly Bible study group. "We don't want to be viewed differently," the wife told me.... As one psychologist put it, "The money taboo is a serious psychological problem because, though we do not talk freely about money, it is of major concern to almost everybody in America."*[150]

The "money taboo" extends beyond instances of financial peril similar to that described by Boss. How are we as Christians

---

150 Boss, Shira. "It's Time to Break the Money Taboo." http://www.beliefnet.com/News/Money/Its-Time-To-Break-The-Money-Taboo.aspx?p=1. Accessed 3/16/15.

encouraging each other in our generosity? The truth is, we aren't. Yet Scripture lays out a clear picture of what living in community with respect to our finances can look like. Acts 2:42-47 demonstrates that openness about our stewardship can be an important driver of life-giving, joyful Christian community. We are not arguing that Christians should necessarily "have all things in common," but rather that sharing in our stewardship can enable us to develop the "glad and generous hearts" of our first-century Christian brothers and sisters in Jerusalem.

Based on our research, we believe that generous stewardship is something best done in community. In this chapter we outline several specific strategies for building a more community-oriented mindset toward our wealth and giving.

FINANCIAL TRANSPARENCY IN ACTION

Hebrews 4:13 (NIV) says that "Nothing in all creation is hidden from God's sight." Many of the generous families with whom we spoke employ some model of financial transparency, and all of them describe it as one of the best decisions they have ever made, both spiritually and financially. Following are three strategies for incorporating financial transparency into our own lives.

PUBLISH AN ANNUAL FINANCIAL REPORT

For the last several years, Brett and Christy Samuels have published an annual financial report and shared it with a set of close friends, mentors, and advisors. The report includes their spending, saving, and serving objectives for the year, an analysis of actual performance relative to those objectives, and stated objectives for the following year. The report includes detail on consumption across key categories, a simplified historical picture of budgets and net worth figures, and an analysis of their giving, including both the amount of and recipients of their giving. The Samuels then speak with each advisor about the report.[151]

Sharing their finances in this way has been incredibly rewarding for the Samuels. Christy says there has been "nothing but benefit in our hearts from being transparent. We are starting to feel more passionate about encouraging others in the same vein."

Brett says the key to success is choosing good advisors. He recommends "selecting people you are actively in community with. Not just all your old friends, but people who see how you're living every day. Also, select people who are thinking about these types of questions as well—who can provide good feedback. Not all financial wizards. We select some pastors—they ask very good questions. Also, we select people across a wide age range, across life stages. You get more wisdom that way." The Samuels also recommend making sure your advisors are committed to the process. "Are they really going to engage, not just consume? Be sure to set expectations." Finally, be sure to set clear objectives for your stewardship. It is only through clear objectives around spending, saving, and serving that your advisors can truly help keep you accountable and offer useful insight or recommendations.

The Samuels have been surprised by the type of advice they have received. For example, one year they cut back significantly on consumption in order to save more money. Upon viewing their financial report, their pastor asked them, "Why do you spend so little on entertainment? Are you serving your marriage well by spending so little?" This was a good reminder for the Samuels that the point of financial transparency is not to enforce some

---

151   Note that the Samuels must maintain an accurate account of their finances in order to create their annual report. Many Christian families do not actually track their spending, saving, or giving. We believe a necessary component of stewardship is to account for the blessings God gives us. How might you feel if you called your asset manager to check on your investments and he responded, "Don't worry about it! They're all growing! Don't be concerned with where they're invested or how much they're worth!"? Simple tools like Mint. com or QuickBooks are great ways to track your stewardship more closely.

sort of pious frugality. This isn't an inquisition on one's spending habits. Rather, it is about acknowledging the role money plays in our faithfulness to Christ across all areas of our lives, and using the wisdom of fellow Christians to improve how we glorify God with our wealth.

FORM A PERSONAL BOARD OF DIRECTORS

Will Pope, owner of the oil and gas company in Oklahoma City, relies on a close group of Christian advisors to guide his stewardship. Will's "Board of Directors" is composed of successful Christian businessmen. Similar to a corporate Board of Directors, Will's Board sets his annual salary. Will's advisors also support him in making difficult financial decisions and provide advice in managing his Personal Wealth Finish Line. Many of the members of Will's Board employ a similar strategy with the same group. They get together at least quarterly, typically at the home of one of the members. The group has grown quite close over time, and they now provide important spiritual counseling to one another across a wide array of life's challenges extending far beyond wealth and money.

We have been greatly blessed by forming a similar group with seven families at Harvard Business School, with a joint commitment to long-term accountability and encouragement. Although we are only one year into the process, we have already received tremendous value from having a Board of Directors for Life ("BoD4L," pronounced "buh-dah-ful") to call upon when serious wisdom is needed or when facing a major decision. The seven husbands hold monthly conference calls where we check-in on each other, asking questions about faith and spiritual discipline, family matters, career development, and financial responsibility. We also make a concerted effort to call, email, or text each other throughout the month to offer encouragement and prayer, or to request advice. John and I have both harnessed the collective wisdom of our group to obtain advice on difficult career decisions even in the first several months of beginning our careers after graduation from business school.

This past fall we held our inaugural BoD4L Annual Meeting. We gathered for three days in the hometown of one of our members. We spent about half our time together doing detailed "performance reviews" on each of our lives. These meetings are by no means harsh or uncomfortable; rather, we provide support, encouragement, and prayer to each other in order to equip each of us to be better husbands, fathers, employees, and most importantly, servants of God. Sitting around the table, one guy remarked, "This is probably a small taste of what Heaven will be like—striving for the greater glory of God, in close community with those who know us well." The other half of our time was spent doing "guy" stuff like grilling meat, playing sports, shooting guns, riding four-wheelers, boasting about our respective high school athletic prowess, etc.—all the activities guys do to bond together! Our goal is to rotate between men-only and family-friendly BoD4L Annual Meetings every other year, ensuring that our wives and children can also experience the incredible Christian community God has provided us through this group.

SHARE WITH YOUR COMMUNITY GROUP

Brandon Fremont, the hedge fund manager from Chicago, relies on his "Community Group" (a.k.a. church small group) for wisdom in financial stewardship. His group employs 100 percent financial transparency with respect to spending, saving, and serving. The group tests each member's thought process on both where and why he is giving, and encourages each individual to make wise choices about consumption. For example, Brandon has counseled a member of his Community Group to forego purchasing a new house that would have stretched the family's finances too thin. But again, the purpose of financial accountability is not to enforce falsely pious frugality. Rather, it is to encourage one another in faithful stewardship. For instance, the group once counseled Brandon not to purchase a $2,000 golf cart he was considering buying, mostly as a toy. In the grand scheme of Brandon's stewardship, $2,000 is fairly insignificant. But he appreciated his group's counsel: "Saving $2,000 on the golf cart felt like faithfulness," he says.

Brandon also reflects on the tremendous value of having those in *close community* know your finances. "It would be easy to find a friend 300 miles away in a similar income bracket to validate your lifestyle. But this is about walking faithfully and being challenged, not just finding comfort from those who look just like you and don't see your daily life."

All of these strategies for introducing financial transparency bring with them a certain level of risk and vulnerability. Bringing up such a sensitive topic within your church community or small group could feel exceedingly difficult—even if your community is otherwise very life-giving to your faith. When I feel this way, I remind myself how influenced I have become by our culture's unwillingness to discuss money (the "money taboo"). There is no inherent reason why discussion of money needs to be kept private within the church, as we see in Acts 2. The excuses we typically give for not discussing money—pride, jealousy, an individualistic entitlement of privacy—provide even more reason to embrace transparency! We are encouraged to be transparent with fellow Christians in many other areas of our lives. Why not be transparent with our finances as well?

COMMUNITY GIVING

Stewardship is typically thought of as a personal responsibility. In a lot of ways, that makes sense—most of us earn wages individually and must think about how to allocate those wages individually, or alongside our spouse if we are married. At the same time, there is great power in doing things in groups. Consider worship at church: the hymns sound *a lot* better when everyone is singing than if I were to sing by myself!

The same can be true of giving. The power of communal giving is demonstrated in Acts 2 and is reiterated by Paul when speaking to the Corinthians about the Macedonians' gift to the Jerusalem church in 2 Corinthians 8. We believe there is significant opportunity to generate higher K_{ROI} through community giving in the Church today. Following are three ideas for what this could look like in your community.

GROUP GIFTS

Matt Mancinelli is EVP of Strategy and Volunteers at Generous Giving. For the last several years, he and three of his friends from college have each contributed a portion of their tithes and offerings to a project to translate the Bible into a new language that will enable missionaries to teach the Gospel to a previously unreached people group. The total cost of the project is $80,000, well beyond what any individual in Matt's group could have contributed on his own. However, because they combined their giving, Matt and his friends were able to undertake such a large-scale project.

John and I are employing a similar strategy with our BoD4L group from Harvard Business School. Our seven families have agreed to designate a portion of our annual giving to a combined fund that will be given as a block gift each year. We plan to do this together for years or even decades to come, learning and iterating our giving model over time. We can do far more and learn far more as a group of 14 than any one couple could on their own. Potential ideas include sponsoring native missionary families in low-income countries, supporting an entire orphanage, funding child discipleship for long-term economic development, or providing scholarships to seminary students in countries with a shortage of biblical teachers. All of these projects would be too big for any one of our families to support individually, but we are excited to tackle one or more of them as a group.

Group giving offers benefits in addition to generating a higher K_{ROI}. When a group of friends are invested in something together, they think about and talk about it more frequently. Think of fans of a professional sports team, for example. In this instance, knowing our friends are also invested in the project will cause us to discuss it with them more often and pray about it more frequently. Whichever project we choose to support will also serve as a great catalyst for our group of friends to spend time together— something that becomes harder to do over time.

While we believe group giving offers many advantages, we also want to clearly state that such initiatives should not come at the expense of supporting your local church and community. Indeed, supporting the local church is the ultimate expression of a "group giving" endeavor.

GIVING MINISTRIES AT LOCAL CHURCHES

Edward and Katherine Heath, from Orange County, believe their spiritual gift is giving generously, per Romans 12:6-8: "We have different gifts, according to the grace given to each of us . . . if it is giving, then give generously" (NIV).

The Heaths thought there ought to be a ministry at their local church specifically designed for people whose spiritual gift is giving. So, they founded the Legacy Dream Team, whose mission is to "serve our church with the Gift of Giving." The Legacy Dream Team "is an outlet for those who are called and equipped to finance the Kingdom of God and to leave a legacy. This team invests in strategic projects in our church, city, state, and nation and in opportunities all around the world." The Legacy Dream Team also provides education on what God says about giving generously and training on how to give effectively. While still relatively new, the ministry has already given extravagantly to an orphanage in Mexico that the church supports and is supporting four other projects, ranging from church-specific infrastructure development to international missions efforts.

The Legacy Dream Team is by no means limited to wealthy members of the church. The invitation to the group reads, "Who can be a part of the Legacy Dream Team? The Legacy Dream Team is for anyone who feels called to give over and above their tithe. There is no specific amount [required] because we consider any amount valuable and precious. As a church we are not built on the gifts and talents of a few, but on the sacrifices of many." Edward says that most of the initial members of the team are business leaders, but the vision is to substantially expand the group over time.

The Legacy Dream Team members' involvement in the projects it supports extends far beyond simply cutting a check. For example, many team members regularly travel to the orphanage in Mexico and oversee its operations. This is a critical feature of the ministry. As we discussed earlier, stewardship does not stop once we have given money: we are also responsible for ensuring the effective utilization of those resources for God's purposes.

Giving ministries need not be specifically targeted to individuals with the spiritual gift of giving. Brandon Fremont, the hedge fund manager from Chicago, launched an adoption ministry at his church that provides financial support to families who desire to adopt but cannot afford to do so. The ministry is funded by any member of the church who wishes to contribute. A selection committee composed of church members reviews applications and allocates the funding. Brandon explains that while he and other donors do sit on the selection committee, the committee also recruits members who are not significant donors to the ministry in order to ensure objectivity when evaluating applications. The ministry has assisted in funding about 12 adoptions to date.

Giving ministries are a great way to enhance the K_{ROI} of church members' "extra" giving beyond typical tithes and offerings. They provide a fantastic channel for those passionate about giving to express their generosity. Finally, they offer a very effective method of educating church members about the joy of generosity and faithful stewardship. Some giving ministries, such as Mission 1:8 at Houston's First Baptist Church in Houston, Texas, are actually coordinated by official church leadership. This can be very effective as well, so long as there is a clear delineation between funding provided to the church's general fund and funding provided to the giving ministry.

If you are passionate about giving we highly recommend launching a similar ministry at your church. Edward and Katherine Heath have graciously agreed to speak with any reader of this book interested in discussing the Legacy Dream Team in more depth. Please contact the authors to be put in touch with the Heaths.

GENEROSITY EDUCATION

We believe giving levels are so low in the Church today partially because of a lack of education about generosity. If the Church invested the same time and energy into educating young men and women on the topic of generosity that it does in educating them on the topics of service or sexual purity, we might see a very different story in the graphs of giving levels today. Even if we are being generous ourselves, *we never talk about it!* How are young people supposed to learn about God's vision for our generosity unless we teach them?

It is true that Jesus calls us to give quietly in Matthew 6:2-4. But He also exhorts us: "In the same way, let your light shine before others, so that they may see your good works and give glory to your Father who is in heaven" (Matthew 5:16). Contrasting these two passages makes clear that the core issue with respect to giving publicly is *motive*. In Matthew 6:2-4, Jesus claims the "hypocrites" give publicly so that "they may be praised by others." In Matthew 5:16, however, we are commanded to do good works publicly so that others may "give glory to your Father . . ." We can honor God by publicly setting an example of generosity, so long as our true motive is to glorify God rather than ourselves.[152]

A significantly underutilized forum for generosity education is mentorship. Many of us have experienced the tremendous value that comes from mentorship—both the wisdom we receive from being mentored and the joy we receive from mentoring others. However, we rarely discuss the topic of stewardship with our mentors. We have again unwittingly subscribed to our culture's "money taboo." But isn't this a huge waste of potential wisdom? Next time we meet with our mentors, we ought to explore how they think about generosity and ask their advice on how we should manage our own stewardship. Similarly, we ought to encourage those whom we are currently mentoring to explore God's Word on the subject and to take actionable steps to fulfill God's vision for their wealth and giving.

Finally, we must be prepared to support a fellow believer who is making poor decisions with respect to his or her stewardship. Paul exhorts us, "Brothers, if anyone is caught in any transgression, you who are spiritual should restore him in a spirit of gentleness. Keep watch on yourself, lest you too be tempted" (Galatians 6:1). Alan Barnhart has said that if he came into church bragging

---

152 Alcorn. *Money, Possessions, and Eternity,* 445.

about cheating on his wife, he would be rightly corrected by his community. But if he spent his vast earning power on himself and made an idol out of wealth, he fears that he might be congratulated on his "success." This should not be so!

Brandon Fremont elaborates on our role in counseling fellow believers in times they may be struggling with their stewardship: "You must model faithfulness, call out faithlessness, and pray for them. But you're not responsible for changing them. You can't take over." There is significant value to be gained in incorporating discussion of generosity into our mentoring relationships and close friendships. But we must be careful not to become like the Pharisees, focusing on "the speck that is in [our] brother's eye, but [not noticing] the log that is in [our] own eye" (Matthew 7:3).

SOLIDARITY WITH OUR FELLOW MAN

As Christ-followers, our community extends beyond our next-door neighbors and beyond the four walls of our local church. While the majority of our time and energy may be spent interacting with those in our local context, we are all but one member of God's global creation. Each of the seven billion humans alive today bears the image of God and has the free offer of His love through Christ. For these reasons alone, our fellow man deserves our dignity and respect.

Maintaining solidarity with our fellow man can be incredibly difficult given that most of us do in fact spend most of our time in our local context. We must never underestimate the extent to which we are influenced by our local culture. Paul warns us in Romans 12:2, "Do not be conformed to this world, but be transformed by the renewal of your mind, that by testing you may discern what is the will of God, what is good and acceptable and perfect." He reiterates in Colossians 2:8, "See to it that no one takes you captive by philosophy and empty deceit, according to human tradition, according to the elemental spirits of the world, and not according to Christ."

Our struggle to heed Paul's warnings is exacerbated by our tendency to constantly compare ourselves to those around us. We conduct both "upward" and "downward" social comparisons. Upward comparisons are made relative to individuals we feel are superior to ourselves in some respect, and vice-versa for downward comparisons. We make upward comparisons in order to motivate ourselves toward self-improvement, or to enhance our self-regard by drawing similarities between ourselves and those in upper social classes. Conversely, we make downward comparisons in order to enhance our self-image relative to those in lower social classes.[153]

Unfortunately, our local context often distorts the scale we use when making these social comparisons.

Figure 6: Our Distorted View of Solidarity

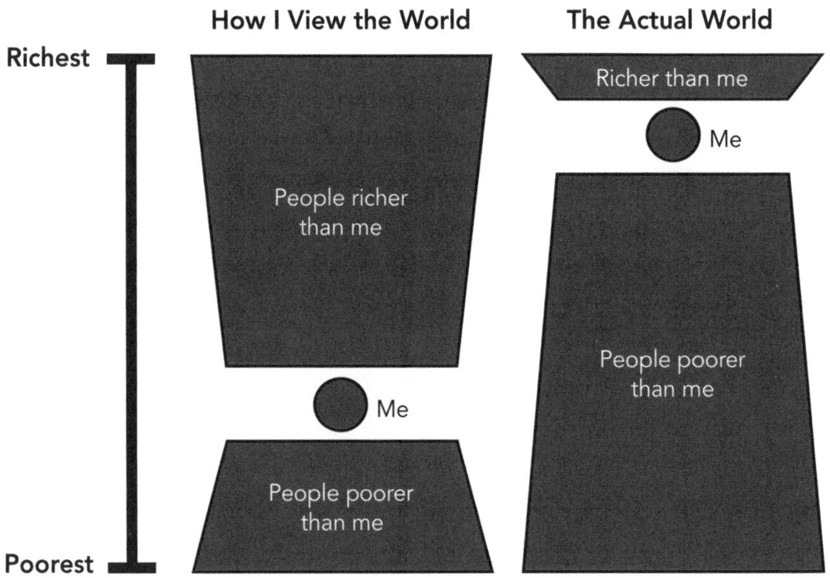

---

153 *Psychology Today.* https://www.psychologytoday.com/basics/social-comparison-theory. Accessed 3/17/15.

Nearly all of us view the world through a distorted lens, as depicted in Figure 6. This is true regardless of our income level. The specific location of "Me" on the right-hand side of the figure will vary according to one's actual income, but in almost all cases, we *think* we are less well-off than we *actually are*. Indeed, an American earning an average individual wage of **$43,000** is two and a half times better off than the global average individual wage of **$18,000**.[154] Keep in mind the $18,000 figure is adjusted for purchasing power parity, so it accounts for differences in the cost of living across countries.

Most of us spend a lot more time conducting "upward" comparisons than "downward" comparisons. This habit foments our culture of materialism—the proverbial "keeping up with the Joneses." We may occasionally take a step back to realize the extent of God's gracious provision in our lives, but within the confines of our gated communities, we spend much of our time admiring our neighbor's new car, comparing technical details of our friend's new entertainment system, subtly dropping comments about our upcoming vacation, or imagining how nice it would be to own our Bible study leader's beautiful wardrobe.

Why is our tendency to compare ourselves "upwards" so dangerous? Why is it so important to maintain solidarity with *all* our fellow men, not just those whom we wish to emulate? The answer is that focusing "upwards" diminishes our ability to truly empathize with "the least of these," which severely restricts our capacity to be generous. Scripture speaks frequently on the importance of empathy: "Bear one another's burdens, and so fulfill the law of Christ" (Galatians 6:2); "Finally, all of you, have unity of mind, sympathy, brotherly love, a tender heart, and a humble mind"

---

154 Alexander, Ruth. "Where are you on the global pay scale?" http://www.bbc.com/news/magazine-17512040. Accessed 3/17/15, and "Per Capita Personal Income by State" https://bber.unm.edu/econ/us-pci.htm. Accessed 3/17/15.

(1 Peter 3:8); "Rejoice with those who rejoice, weep with those who weep" (Romans 12:15) and of course the classic Golden Rule, "So whatever you wish that others would do to you, do also to them, for this is the Law and the Prophets" (Matthew 7:12).

Failing to empathize restricts our generosity in several ways. First, focusing upwards causes us to underestimate the need to be generous. The relative wealth of our local context blinds us to the tremendous needs of those outside our local context. Consider the Rich Man's treatment of Lazarus in Luke 16. John and I were frightened by how much more we relate to the rich man than to Lazarus. While many of us may not *feel* rich, we often wear "fine linens" whose value could supply an entire wardrobe for an underprivileged child, and frequently enjoy "sumptuous meals" whose cost could feed a needy family for a week.

Second, failing to empathize reduces the effectiveness of our generosity even when we do recognize the need to be generous. Recall Denise Whitfield's experience with wealthy members of her church who attempted to help her family during a period of financial need. Denise's friends meant well, but because of their inability to empathize with Denise's situation they were not able to effectively support her.

Perhaps the most dangerous aspect of these phenomena is that we frequently don't even realize they are happening! Brandon Fremont comments, "our community is wealthy, so [we have] the real fear that we won't realize it if the water we are in is starting to boil." Brandon and his family actively work to maintain empathy with *all* of God's children by investing in relationships with families across the entire socioeconomic spectrum. For example, their Community Group has included high-, medium-, and low-income families, and they have invested significant time in working with orphanage ministries both in the U.S. and abroad.

Some people think that intentionally "working" to maintain empathy is somehow insincere or compromised by an ulterior motive. We disagree! If we are not intentional, the natural gravity of our lives pulls us toward others similar to ourselves and away from those for whom it is critical we maintain genuine empathy. Further, note that empathy is not synonymous with pity. Being generous out of true empathy offers to others the dignity and respect they deserve; being generous out of pity introduces a hierarchical, transactional nature to the relationship, even if done unintentionally. Paul beautifully articulates our need to maintain empathy in 1 Corinthians 9:19-23.

> *For though I am free from all, I have made myself a servant to all, that I might win more of them. To the Jews I became a Jew . . . to those under the law I became as one under the law . . . to those outside the law I became as one outside the law . . . to the weak I became weak, that I might win the weak. I have become all things to all people, that by all means I might save some. I do it all for the sake of the Gospel, that I may share with them in its blessings.*

Ultimately, we seek to empathize with our fellow man for the sake of the Gospel and as a result of the Gospel in us.

Finally, we want to point out that maintaining empathy does not necessitate that we feel guilty for the blessings God has given us. We may feel guilty if we have hoarded those blessings for ourselves rather than used them for God's purposes, but in that case the guilt is centered not on God's provision but rather on our response to it. Scripture makes clear that God delights in blessing us, and that His provision, even in abundance, is rightly counted as blessing.[155] So we need not feel guilty merely for the fact that God, in His sovereignty, has blessed us with much. Instead, we ought to praise God for his tremendous provision, and then embrace the responsibility to be generous with that provision.[156]

For a Closer Look . . .

Tom and Bree Hsieh are a great example of living Kingdom-oriented lives while maintaining solidarity with all people. Despite a windfall received in a tech IPO, they have lived a very modest life, deeply integrated into the lower-income community where they have chosen to live in order to have greater ministry opportunities.

See their story in this seven-minute video, "Into the Neighborhood," at GodandMoney.net/resources.

Edward and Katherine Heath have thought a lot about this topic. Katherine says, "We don't have a lot of guilt associated with our expectation of God's blessing. There is no logical reason why God has blessed us so much—blessing on top of blessing. It's just crazy what He does! On the other hand, my brother has an incredible heart for God—he serves, tithes, gives—and yet it seems like nothing goes right for him. He has experienced serious injuries, job loss . . . just recently he had a serious car wreck. I have prayed a lot about this, and the response I've heard from God is, 'That's not your concern.' Disparity is a tough, tough question. But in Genesis 12:2 we see we are 'blessed to be a blessing.' If God has blessed us, we know for a fact it is to be a blessing to others. We've learned not to get beat up about the fact that we're blessed. We just choose to be generous with what we have."

---

155 Proverbs 3:9-10; Malachi 3:10; Luke 6:38, etc.

156 1 Chronicles 29; 2 Corinthians 9: 12-13

We believe there is great value in making our stewardship more of a community activity. Through financial transparency, group giving projects, and local giving ministries, we can leverage the collective power of our fellow brothers and sisters in Christ to generate significantly higher K_{ROI} for God. By incorporating stewardship into our small groups and mentoring relationships, we can drastically improve the education and shared wisdom on the subject of generosity in our churches. By maintaining solidarity with our fellow man, we maintain the necessary empathy to recognize the need for generosity and the ability to formulate an effective response to that need. We believe the potential exists to unleash a powerful surge in generosity across the "Capital-C-Church" through combining financial forces to make an impact for God's Kingdom!

CHAPTER TEN

Our Conclusions

"How we view money is indicative of where we've placed our faith and trust. If you want to grow in your faith, wrestle with stewardship."

—Brandon Fremont

Our primary objective at the beginning of this project was simply to think about how to manage wealth and giving in our own lives. As graduate students with limited net worth but with expectations of future earnings, we wanted to "get ahead" of the money, so to speak. As Al Mueller, President of Excellence in Giving, told us, it's a lot easier to form habits of generous living *before* the money is actually in your bank account!

By God's grace, what was intended to be a simple study to inform our own personal giving habits grew to be so much more than that. What was supposed to be a 30-page term paper became an 80-page white paper. The 80-page white paper then became this book (it's like the Lord of the Rings movies—it never ends!). So, we thought we would recap our key findings as a way to concisely summarize the whole project.

THE BIBLE OFFERS A CLEAR AND CONSISTENT NARRATIVE ON WEALTH AND GIVING.

God's overall story is one of faithfulness, salvation, and grace. But He also says a lot about money—over 2,000 verses, in fact! God weaves a clear and consistent narrative about wealth and giving throughout His Word. We often miss this because we do not typically study the specific subject of money longitudinally through Scripture. Performing this type of longitudinal study allows us to accurately piece together God's key lessons on wealth and generosity.

OUR WEALTH HAS A PURPOSE, AND IT IS NOT THE ENDLESS PURSUIT OF *MORE*.

Many of us live under the assumption that the purpose of our money is to increase our quality of life, even if we never explicitly articulate it that way. God sees things differently. Our wealth is a blessing from Him, and is given to us so that we might bless others. In other words, our possessions should be used for Kingdom purposes. This line of thinking is in accord with *our* overall purpose: "To glorify God, and to enjoy Him forever."[157] As stewards, our role is to actively and responsibly manage God's creation for God's purposes. Our wealth is but one tool by which we pursue this objective.

ADOPTING AN ABUNDANCE MINDSET OFFERS A LEVEL OF JOY AND SATISFACTION WE COULD NOT OTHERWISE HOPE TO ACHIEVE.

To embrace a mindset of abundance is to trust in God for our provision, offer gratitude for His blessings, and generously share those blessings with others. Living with a mindset of abundance allows us to experience a joy far greater than we could ever hope to

---

157 From the Westminster Shorter Catechism. http://www.westminsterconfession.org/confessional-standards/the-westminster-shorter-catechism.php. Accessed 3/4/15.

achieve by fearfully accumulating assets under a scarcity mindset. We find true happiness in our money only when we share it with others, not when we keep it for ourselves. As the saying goes, "Money is like manure. When you pile it up, it stinks. But if you spread it around, it can do some good."

GENEROSITY IS BEST DONE IN COMMUNITY.

We often leverage our combined talents to accomplish great things in God's name—for example, praising God through corporate worship or hosting a vacation Bible study for children. However, generosity has often been viewed as a private, individual matter. This should change—we can amplify our K_{ROI} by being generous as a community. Financial transparency, group giving, local giving ministries, church-wide initiatives, and generosity-focused mentorship allow us to leverage our collective generosity to more effectively serve God's Kingdom.

WE MUST MAINTAIN SOLIDARITY WITH OUR FELLOW HUMAN BEINGS IN ORDER TO BE EFFECTIVE STEWARDS.

All seven billion humans alive today bear the image of God, and therefore deserve our dignity and respect. Because we spend so much time in our own local context and are so prone to comparing ourselves "upwards," we often fail to maintain empathy for those outside our local context. Maintaining empathy is critical because it enables us to better appreciate the need for and improve the effectiveness of our generosity. Empathy is not synonymous with pity—we are called to maintain the honor and dignity of our fellow man through our generosity. At the same time, we need not feel guilty about God's provision in our lives, for God receives glory and pleasure in blessing us. Disparity is a difficult issue. We may not be able to resolve disparity, but we can respond to God's abundant provision by being sacrificially generous with whatever blessings God has provided.

IT IS POSSIBLE TO DEVELOP A COHERENT FRAMEWORK FOR MODERN-DAY MANAGEMENT OF WEALTH AND GIVING.

Many resources on Christian giving focus on our "heart for generosity" rather than offering specific advice on managing wealth and giving. Rightly so—it is ultimately our heart that Christ will judge, and ours is a faith based on grace, not works. However, this approach often leaves a gap between the theoretical orientation of our hearts and the actual decisions we make in our real lives each day. We acknowledge the primacy of the heart, but also strongly believe that actions matter, and amounts matter! Christians are called to be generous stewards, and that implies real action. We suspect that "I did not feel led to give" will not stand as a reasonable defense when Jesus questions our giving habits. Sometimes we need a more detailed, specific plan on how to move toward a generous life than "focus on your heart."

This project equipped us to develop a coherent framework for managing spending, saving, and serving in our own lives. Rather than being prescriptive, we hope this framework offers a way of pegging your own tendencies as a Spender, Saver, or Servant, and then embarking on a journey of growth toward more Christ-like financial management decisions. Financial Finish Lines, while not a requirement of Scripture by any means, appear to us as a best practice for combating the human tendency to always thirst for more and more self-gratification.

TOO MANY CHRISTIANS ASK, "HOW MUCH SHOULD I GIVE?" THE RIGHT QUESTION IS, "HOW MUCH DO I NEED TO KEEP?"

Many Christians determine their level of giving based on how much they believe they must give in order to obey God. We argue that these individuals are thinking about the question backward!

Embracing the notion that everything we have truly belongs to God leads instead to the question, "How much do I really need to keep?" Truly embracing God's sovereignty over our lives and genuinely trusting in Him for our provision leads to the natural conclusion that we can honor Him by humbly providing for ourselves and generously giving away the rest!

THE FINAL CONCLUSION

Our final conclusion is a bit different from the rest. It is not theoretical, philosophical, or theological. Instead, it is social: **we learned that regular people are really doing this!** Below we describe our key findings from the many interactions we shared with incredibly generous men and women of God throughout this project.

We were very fortunate to speak with many individuals who are honoring God in radical ways with their wealth and giving, including Brandon Fremont, Will and Rachel Pope, Denise Whitfield, Brett and Christy Samuels, and Edward and Katherine Heath. We learned, though, that these individuals are just the tip of the iceberg. There are many thousands of other Christians living radically generous lives around the world today. Some of them are wealthy, but most are not. Most of them are regular individuals whose lives have been transformed by Christ's gift of salvation through grace. What makes them unique is their response to that gift: they have embraced the joy that comes from a life spent serving Christ in gratitude for His sacrifice. Generous giving is but one way that they serve Him.

We sought to understand two specific factors with respect to these individuals' inspiring levels of generosity, with the hope that we could emulate such practices in our own lives:

■ What causes someone to become radically generous?

■ What tactical, day-to-day beliefs or behaviors fuel their generosity over time?

WHAT CAUSES SOMEONE TO BECOME RADICALLY GENEROUS?

Our research reveals three primary catalysts for embracing a lifestyle of radical generosity. First is a deep understanding of God's Word on the subject. We hope Chapter One offered some insight into God's vision for our wealth and giving. For further reading, we recommend *Money, Possessions, and Eternity* and *The Treasure Principle*, both by Randy Alcorn, and *When Helping Hurts* by Brian Fikkert and Steve Corbett.

Second is direct exposure to the joy that comes from a life of generosity. This exposure is often gained through relationships with close friends or fellow church members who are living very generous lives. We recommend seeking counsel from those in your network whom you know to be honoring God with their wealth and giving. Invite them to dinner and pick their brain on why and how they live this way, as well as what the results have been with respect to their faith and overall happiness. We also recommend exploring several organizations whose mission is to support Christians seeking to enhance their generosity, including the National Christian Foundation, Generous Giving, and Compass—Finances God's Way.

Third is firsthand experience or observation of the deep need for generosity in our broken, sinful world. Sometimes this occurs in our own lives during times of struggle. Other times we experience the need for generosity through the lives of others. This is why it is so important we maintain empathy for our fellow man. We recommend getting involved in a local ministry that supports individuals well outside your local context, participating in an international mission trip, or visiting missionaries supported by your local church.

WHAT TACTICAL, DAY-TO-DAY BELIEFS OR BEHAVIORS FUEL GENEROSITY OVER TIME?

Once someone has embraced a lifestyle of radical generosity, how do they sustain it over time? We again observed three key factors. First, these individuals view their money and possessions as truly belonging to God. This is not some trite Christian cliché—they genuinely believe it. This belief makes the decision to be generous much easier, and is often expressed tactically through caps on spending and/or saving (i.e., financial finish lines). It's the daily answer to the question, "How much do I need to keep?" We recommend thinking about how much money you really need to keep, and imagining what it might look like to give back to God everything you earn beyond that figure.

Second, these individuals have a very high level of expectancy around the joy they will receive from being generous. Katherine Heath describes this expectancy as a fundamental belief that God will deliver on His promises.[158] They have fully bought into the notion that being generous will make them better off in the long-run—perhaps not financially, but certainly in levels of joy and satisfaction. That said, several individuals attribute much of the increase in provision they have received in their lives to their willingness to be generous with smaller levels of provision in the past. This is not a give-to-get attitude, but rather a recognition that God may choose to pour resources onto those whom He knows will steward them wisely. It does not take long for these individuals to move from an expectancy of joy based on faith to an expectancy of joy based on actual prior experience: once they have experienced the joy of generosity firsthand, they seek to experience it again and again.

Finally, we observed that these individuals' generosity is rooted in their overall deep faith in Christ. That is to say, generosity

---

158 Malachi 3:10; Proverbs 3:9-10; Luke 6:38, etc.

is simply one component of their transformed life in Christ. Surprisingly, the causal influence seems to work both ways: while their generosity has certainly grown as they've deepened in their faith, their faith has also deepened as they've taken intentional steps to increase their generosity. We observed several individuals take bold, scary steps into generosity—and God met them there. God's faithfulness then fueled their generosity even more. In other words, our faith and our finances are inextricably linked. This observation has encouraged us to take bold steps in our own generosity, even if we do not yet feel we have a strong enough faith to back this up.

God blessed this project in amazing ways throughout its duration. He continually pushed us, revealed new insights to us, opened doors for us, and introduced us to amazing individuals who are passionately serving Christ through their generosity. Most importantly, He changed our hearts. We came to understand much more deeply that stewardship is but one component of our faithful response to Christ for His eternal and priceless gift of salvation through grace. We learned that generosity is the joyful response of a heart that has been transformed by Christ's redemptive love. Rather than seeing giving as a personal challenge, like dieting or weight loss, we have come to see it as a gift, as an opportunity to participate in the fulfillment of God's purposes on Earth. This book is about money, to be sure, but undergirding all of that is God's story of redemption, salvation, and grace. Making this connection crystal clear in our minds is one of the greatest blessings God has given us through this project.

As we continued to work on this book, our vision for generosity in the "Capital-C-Church" grew as well. We learned that there is significant interest in the Church today on the topic of generosity. Many of us think regularly about how to serve God with the abundant resources with which He has blessed us, but we aren't sure how to do it. However, we believe momentum is growing. Several professionals who have studied Christian generosity for many years told us that excitement around the topic of generosity is at the highest level they have ever seen. We believe God is beginning to mobilize His Church to launch a wave of generosity never before experienced on Earth.

Our vision is that the radical levels of generosity exhibited by the individuals in this book become commonplace—that more and more Christians, regardless of income level, choose to live their lives with a mindset of joyful abundance, all the while offering gratitude to God for His provision and serving Him generously with their wealth. Our prayer is that millions of Spenders and Savers become Servants to Christ as they experience His redemptive grace in their financial lives. Every follower of Christ who chooses to live this way glorifies God and increases the impact and influence of God's Kingdom here on Earth.

So we pose our final question to you: how much do you really need to keep?

For a Closer Look . . .

When you finish reading this book, don't let it be the end of your exploration about this topic . . . let it be the beginning. See Appendix A for a reading list of outstanding resources. Appendix B describes the very best groups we know of that can help you discover how to live a God-honoring, generous life. There are others like you—people who love Jesus and want to honor Him in generous stewardship. You can find them through these organizations! So . . . what's next for you? Let Generous Giving help you host a Journey of Generosity for your friends. Call up a Kingdom Advisor. Open a Giving Fund. Form a personal board of directors. Ask the Lord right now what He might have you do as a next step!

EPILOGUE

Where Are We Now?

"Our view of God is such that we know we can trust Him implicitly."
—Bill Bright, Founder of Campus Crusade for Christ

God taught us so much through the creation of this book. Yet, we were both shocked by how quickly He asked each of us to put what we learned into practice! Following is a brief update on our lives over the past year, spanning from the beginning of this project to the book's completion. We share this in order to highlight God's faithfulness, as well as to reflect in gratitude on the fact that our all-powerful God chooses to use every one of us, mere sinners, to build His Kingdom.

EXPOSING HIDDEN SIN (WRITTEN BY GREG)

Before graduate school, John and I both tithed regularly. But just like the Pharisees in Matthew 23, our easy, black-and-white obedience to tithing was actually masking hidden sin with respect to our stewardship. John was a Saver, and I was a Spender. As a

Saver, John was prone to idolatry, attaching safety and security to his growing net worth instead of his Savior. As a Spender, I was prone to materialism, placing greater value in created goods than in my Creator. We were each missing the point!

Professor Cox's "God and Money" course at Harvard Divinity School was the first step in our journey toward becoming Servants. It didn't take us long, sitting in Professor Cox's classroom, to realize that God had an altogether different vision for our money and possessions than we did. But it took us the entire semester (. . . and the following semester . . . and almost an entire year after graduation, up until this writing) to figure out exactly what that vision was. Even as we were writing a book about becoming Servants, there remained a disconnect between our intellectual understanding of God's expectations for our stewardship and our actual, day-to-day experiences.

Given how frequently God taught important lessons to biblical characters through their real-life experiences, perhaps we should have seen His next moves coming. Of course, we didn't. It turns out that even in the months following completion of this text, God had big plans to stretch our faith and our generosity through His work in our lives.

THE HOLIEST JOB—MINISTRY OR MARKETPLACE? (WRITTEN BY GREG)

The first signal of things to come was an exciting email that John and I received on a snowy winter day in Boston. Todd Harper, President of Generous Giving (GG), wanted to meet us! You may recall that we conducted a survey of 200-plus business leaders as part of our final term paper for the "God and Money" course. In their responses, many of these individuals touted Generous Giving as a fantastic organization doing amazing work in spreading the message of biblical generosity. Several people recommended we contact GG as part of our project. Despite deploying our best networking skills, however, we were failing to make any headway in connecting with GG. So what a surprise to find an email from GG's president in our inboxes!

Soon after, we met Todd Harper and Matt Mancinelli from GG for lunch in Boston. Todd and Matt cast an inspiring vision for the work God is doing to ignite greater levels of generosity in His Church. Todd actually offered us jobs with GG during our meeting. It was a tempting offer (in a good way). I'll always remember Todd's closing pitch: "There are trillions of dollars locked up in Christians' bank accounts today. No matter how much you could ever hope to earn and give away personally, the sum pales in comparison to the impact you could have by helping others experience the joy of generosity."

The problem was that I was already deeply imbedded into a healthcare technology startup in Nashville, Tennessee. I had actually spent the prior summer interning with the company, called naviHealth, and was working for naviHealth part-time throughout my final year of graduate school. Following our lunch with Todd and Matt, I was so inspired by the possibility of serving God in ministry as a member of GG; yet, I was equally excited by the opportunities I had waiting for me at naviHealth. My wife, Alison, and I spent many pre-bedtime prayers inquiring God on what we should do. Alison was highly supportive either way (as you can tell, she's awesome). But I was torn. Given everything God had taught me through the writing of this book, didn't it make sense that I should go share those same lessons with others? Would I be committing a "Jonah" by going into the private sector?

Over time, and through much thought, reflection, and prayer, I came to the conclusion that a career in the private sector can be just as holy as a career in ministry. It's all about motive. I learned a lot by reading through The Theology of Work Project's website and by studying Scripture.[159] Two verses that really impacted me were Colossians 3:17 ("And whatever you do, in word or deed, do everything in the name of the Lord Jesus, giving thanks to God the Father through Him") and Matthew 5:16 ("In the same way, let your light shine before others, so that they may see your good works and give glory to your Father who is in heaven").

God views work as a good thing. As long as I show up at the office every day with the objective of using the skills and gifts God has given me to glorify Him, both through my work itself and through my interactions with others, He is pleased. As I gained confidence in this perspective through conversations with other Christians whom I trust, the decision to join naviHealth became clearer.

FREEDOM IN BOUNDARIES
(WRITTEN BY JOHN)

While Greg was experiencing God's confirmation in his path to the marketplace, I was experiencing God's challenge and call to ministry. C. S. Lewis famously said that he was the most dejected and reluctant convert in all of England when he came to the Lord. I think I may have been the most dejected and reluctant ministry worker in the history of ministry!

It started with Chevron pulling the plug on my dream job—in Perth, Australia—a few short days before our initial lunch meeting with Todd Harper. I still had a slot in a highly compelling expatriate rotational program, but I had negotiated and maneuvered for over a year to skip the rotations and jump right in on the second largest oil and gas project in the world, praying for God's will all the while. We were looking at houses there, investigating schools,

---

159 www.thetheologyofwork.org

and planning to stay for up to a decade in the land down under. Long story short, it fell through—on my wife Megan's birthday, to make matters worse! This put me back in an open pool of potential positions worldwide. (I even had a *backup* job in Perth, which also fell through in the same week.) Frustrated and feeling dislocated, when Todd offered us jobs my response was, "a week ago I would have laughed at you. I don't know what this means, but I'm not laughing."

A season of fasting and praying ensued, in which I felt God lead me toward the Generous Giving opportunity. I felt a strong burden to advance the prophetic mission in which this organization is engaged, to speak a word to our modern culture about the grace of giving. I had an immovable knot in my stomach over this. Megan and I would put our kids to bed, lay down for the night, and cry our eyes out. Why would God give us a dream (to become expatriate workers for Chevron), let us spend five years pursuing it, and then ask us to lay it down at the moment of consummation? Why would we take out student loans in a plan to double our income, then intentionally take a job with *lower* income? I was literally deferring phone calls from my Chevron relocation consultant who stood ready to send the moving trucks—it was that down-to-the-wire. We explicitly discussed saying no to the Lord, going overseas, and living the way we wanted to. (Jonah, if he could advise us, would probably say this was a bad idea given his incident with the whale.)

We prayed that God would make it crystal-clear if He wanted us to change course in life. Much to our chagrin, He did. A missionary friend far overseas, who had no specific knowledge of my circumstances, sent me an email telling me that he didn't know why, but God had put me on his heart, and I was probably supposed to leave Chevron and pursue something else after graduation. My mom had a dream that she shared with me that she felt like was from God, that suggested I ought to consider a new path in my life. A professional investor and Harvard graduate asked to speak with me on the phone, saying that he felt burdened to share a story with me—a story of his classmate who had left the private sector to work in ministry after finishing at Harvard Business School. We continued to wrestle with the decision, listening to "Oceans" by Hillsong on repeat, probably over 100 times. The song speaks of trusting God deeply, and stepping into a place where reliance upon Him is required.

Megan and I prayerfully considered how low of a salary we could take at this stage of life in going into ministry. Our number was 60 to 70 percent lower than what we'd have been making at Chevron, but it was probably aggressively high for a nonprofit, to be honest. (Given that we had already decided to give away 50 percent of our first year's pay at Chevron as an experiment in radical generosity, this salary range seemed like something we could handle.) With student loans and a growing family we asked God to confirm our calling by making my salary situation work out. I did not share the number with anyone but Megan. When we got down to numbers, Generous Giving offered me precisely the salary Megan and I had settled on—to the dollar.

In my prior mindset, I never could have accepted the offer. Why would I earn less and sacrifice millions of dollars from my potential net worth, guaranteeing that I'd have to work well past my planned retirement age of 40? However, setting finish lines and establishing boundaries in my life gave me the ultimate freedom to be able to make such a choice. With a fixed lifestyle in mind, regardless of my earning power, and a desire to work my entire adult life anyway, why not follow the Lord into ministry? The choice was still hard, but it had become possible.

The President of Harvard, when conferring degrees upon the Law School students at graduation, says this: "May you go forth and wisely interpret those constraints which keep us free." To be free, as a society, we must have laws—boundaries and constraints which govern our free behavior. Anarchy would be anything but freedom! Our financial lives are no different. By taking up rules for myself to honor the Lord, I gained the freedom to follow Him. Indeed, as C. S. Lewis went on to reflect after his own conversion, "[God's] compulsion is our liberation."

God Owns It All
(written by Greg)

Six weeks after I joined naviHealth full-time, we were acquired by Cardinal Health, a giant healthcare company in Ohio, for over $400 million. My first thought was, "Ah, I see what you did there, God!" I was so inspired by John's choice to join Generous Giving and was so excited by the amazing opportunities John was receiving to share God's message of biblical generosity. On the other hand, while confident in my decision to enter the private sector, I was beginning to wonder if my part in this story was coming to an end.

Once the naviHealth/Cardinal Health transaction occurred, however, it was clear that God still had plans for me. I was fortunate to own a portion of the equity in naviHealth, which meant that I received a sizable cash windfall as a result of the transaction. I received some of the cash up front, while the remainder was reinvested into naviHealth. The total payout was in the mid-six-figures, and could eclipse seven figures if naviHealth continues to grow quickly over the next few years. Here I was, six weeks into my new job, having just completed this manuscript, and God provided me a real-life "test" of sorts. Did I learn anything, after all?

I am thankful to God for Alison's and my response to this windfall. First, we immediately and continually thanked God for His abundant provision. Rather than taking personal credit for the payout, we heaped praise on our Lord for His generous gift.

Second, we excitedly made plans to give away a significant portion of the proceeds (about 20 percent), rather than making plans to immediately spend it. The remainder is mostly allocated to various savings goals, from paying down student loans to putting a down payment on a home. Having already decided "how much we need to keep" by establishing Lifestyle Limits, the choice of how much to give was actually fairly easy—and very freeing. In the past, we would have immediately begun planning for a larger home or for our next international luxury vacation (not that there's anything wrong with vacation!). Instead, we were having *more fun* praying about creative avenues God might open for us to serve Him!

Third, we were blessed with community with which we could engage in discussions about how to best utilize these funds. I spent time with several members of our Board of Directors for Life to obtain their advice and wisdom. This was extremely helpful in terms of receiving both tactical advice on Spend-vs.-Save-vs.-Serve decisions and deeper spiritual accountability from fellow followers of Christ.

To be clear, I give all the credit for Alison's and my changed hearts to Christ. I *know* I would have responded differently to this situation just a few months prior. I am very thankful for His provision of financial resources, but am even more grateful for His provision of wisdom on how to manage those resources. Most importantly, I now know that it's all His to begin with!

THE FAITHFULNESS OF GOD (WRITTEN BY JOHN)

After taking the job with Generous Giving, Megan and I began experiencing His grace and provision in many ways. We still have our struggles, and there are days when we question our choice, question God's faithfulness, and even question whether we should have just followed our own plans rather than His. The tears we cried when making our decision were not the last ones, and many more came in the process of adjusting to our new lives. But we trust in His goodness, we trust that we're accumulating treasure in heaven, and we trust that He holds our present and future in His hands.

We were abundantly blessed to acquire our home, a 2,500 square foot, four bedroom house with a view of a community pond. It's beautiful, and the sun rises over the pond every morning, showering us with the golds, pinks, and blues of a Florida sunrise. We feel God's grace toward us in raising our children there. However, the down payment required us to deploy almost all liquid assets we had at our disposal. With a growing family and only one car in our possession, we knew we'd need another vehicle very soon.

We had long pined after a minivan for its practicality and interior space. (Fellow parents will recognize this stage of life, and also share our conviction that the Honda Odyssey is the unchallenged queen of minivans!) We wanted a new Odyssey, but committed to not take out a car loan. In one of my first weeks on the job, a fellow Generous Giving employee said this to a few of us: "Guys, can you pray for me? I have this old Honda Odyssey, with 160,000 miles, and it's time to get rid of it. It runs like a champ, but we're past that stage of life. I've been wanting to sell it for four months but I don't have peace about it, and the Holy Spirit hasn't let me do it. I'm not sure what to do." Naturally, I spoke up, and bought his van! After paying the fair price for the car, we had just a few thousand dollars of liquidity left in our lives. God had provided for us within our circumstances.

I cannot describe the rich sense of joy on Megan's face as she sat in that minivan in July, 2015. After shuttling our family in a sedan, sometimes carrying suitcases on our lap because there wasn't enough room in the trunk, we had a vehicle with space for so much more! But God wasn't done showing us His love. He had heard us crying out to Him in Boston as we wrestled with our decision, and He must have taken note of the song playing in the background as we did so. The first time Megan started the van, after putting the kids in their car seats, she turned on the radio. You can guess which song was playing . . .

"Oceans."

In that moment, it was as if God was speaking to Megan, telling her that He would be faithful to provide for her needs as she continued to follow Him.

PARTING THOUGHTS

God has given us challenges in the past year, which we now have realized were opportunities to grow in our trust in His goodness and provision. As a pastor out in West Texas said to John one time, "You never know what lies on the other side of obedience." We're thankful to have shared our story with more than 10,000 people thus far, with more opportunities to do so scheduled, and we look forward to seeing what He has planned for the years to come. All of this has come as a pleasant surprise, and we give God 100 percent of the credit and glory for the journey.

We don't know what God has planned for you, or even what He has in the future for us. But we do know, through our experiences over the past year, that He is radically generous, limitless in His love, and He will take us beyond our comfort zone if we let Him. Will you give Him your financial life, and see what He might do?

Appendix A: Further Reading

Alcorn, Randy C. *Money, Possessions, and Eternity.* Wheaton, IL: Tyndale House, 2003.

Alcorn, Randy C. *The Treasure Principle.* Sisters, Or.: Multnomah, 2001.

Blomberg, Craig. *Neither Poverty nor Riches: A Biblical Theology of Material Possessions.* Grand Rapids, MI: Eerdmans, 1999.

Carnegie, Andrew. "The Gospel of Wealth," *The Gospel of Wealth, and Other Timely Essays.* Garden City, NY: Doubleday, Doran & Co., 1933.

Corbett, Steve, and Brian Fikkert. *When Helping Hurts: How to Alleviate Poverty without Hurting the Poor—and Yourself.* Chicago, IL: Moody Publishers, 2009.

Croteau, David A. *You Mean I Don't Have to Tithe?: A Deconstruction of Tithing and a Reconstruction of Post-tithe Giving.* Eugene, Or.: Wipf and Stock Pub., 2010.

Dunn, Elizabeth, and Michael I. Norton. *Happy Money: The New Science of Smarter Spending.* New York, NY: Simon & Schuster, 2013.

Keller, Timothy, and Katherine Leary Alsdorf. *Every Good Endeavour: Connecting Your Work to God's Plan for the World.* New York, NY: Dutton, 2012.

Manion, Jeff. *Satisfied: Discovering Contentment in a World of Consumption.* Grand Rapids, MI: Zondervan, 2013.

McClanen, Don and Dale Stitt. "Ministry of Money." Faith and Money Network. http://faithandmoneynetwork.org/.

Piketty, Thomas and Arthur Goldhammer. *Capital in the Twenty-first Century.* Cambridge, MA: Harvard University Press, 2014.

Plummer, Robert L. *40 Questions about Interpreting the Bible.* Grand Rapids, MI: Kregel Publications, 2010.

Simon, Arthur. *How Much is Enough? Hungering for God in an Affluent Culture.* Grand Rapids, MI: Baker Books, 2003

Smith, Christian, and Hilary A. Davidson. *The Paradox of Generosity: Giving We Receive, Grasping We Lose.* New York, NY: Oxford University Press, 2014.

Smith, Christian, Michael O. Emerson, and Patricia Snell. *Passing the Plate: Why American Christians Don't Give Away More Money.* Oxford: Oxford University Press, 2008.

Stanley, Andy. *Fields of Gold: A Place beyond Your Deepest Fears, a Prize beyond Your Wildest Imagination.* Wheaton, IL: Tyndale House Publishers, 2004.

Tierney, Thomas J., and Joel L. Fleishman. *Give Smart: Philanthropy That Gets Results.* New York: PublicAffairs, 2011.

Appendix B: Additional Resources

Organization	Core Offering(s)	Your Next Step
Generous Giving www.generousgiving.org	Journey of Generosity overnight retreat Celebration of Generosity annual conference	Register for the Annual Celebration of Generosity, or sign up to host a Journey of Generosity for your friends (they can provide a trained facilitator and there is no cost to you).
National Christian Foundation www.nationalchristian.com	Donor-advised funds. It's like a giving checking account—your own miniature family foundation, from which you can control all of your giving.	Consider opening a Giving Fund, especially if you would like to explore tax-advantaged gifts of appreciated assets, business equity, land, etc. Or, get coffee with a representative from your local NCF office to learn more.
Kingdom Advisors www.kingdomadvisors.com	Network of financial advisors who are trained and committed to a biblical view of money and wealth. They can take you beyond spreadsheets and goals, and explore the heart issues around money.	Find a local CKA—Certified Kingdom Advisor—and consider meeting with them.
Women Doing Well www.womendoingwell.org	Seminars for women to discover their giving purpose, passion, and plan. City-focused one-day events to build communities of women empowered to live in the fullness of their giftings for God's kingdom.	Check out their website for an event near you or to get connected.
Compass Ministries www.compass1.org	Biblical education on money and wealth. Practical resources to equip you to become both generous and wise in your handling of finances.	Register for or sign up to host a small group study.